D1737863

THE TANTRIC PILLOW BOOK

THE TANTRIC PILLOW BOOK

101 Nights of Sexual Ecstasy

CASSANDRA LORIUS

Thorsons
An Imprint of HarperCollins*Publishers*
77–85 Fulham Palace Road,
Hammersmith, London W6 8JB

The website address is:
www.thorsonselement.com

and *Thorsons* are trademarks of
HarperCollins*Publishers* Limited

Originally published as *101 Nights of Tantric Sex*
This edition published by Thorsons 2004

1 3 5 7 9 10 8 6 4 2

A catalogue record of this book
is available from the British Library

ISBN 0 00 717487 X

Printed and bound in Thailand by Imago

CONTENTS

INTRODUCTION

Tantra literally means a "tool for expansion": *tan* translates as "weaving" and "expansion", and *tra* as "tool". Tantras are texts outlining rituals for spiritual transformation. As a practice, Tantra promotes expansion on an energetic, psychological, and physical level, through weaving together different energy processes in the body. A Tantric approach to life means that this flowing together of physical, erotic and spiritual energies is consciously acknowledged.

In spite of the eastern terminology, Tantra is an easy concept to grasp. At its heart is the knowledge that a powerful current of energy flows through us all, which needs to be harmonized.

The practical techniques in this book are intended to cultivate sexual energy, and use it to power inner transformation. In this way, you can give your love-making its full importance by making it into a ritual that you can play with, explore, and develop.

An Eastern path of self-development, Tantra was known as the Tao of Love in China, because it sees sexual energy as just one manifestation of our life force. In the West, however, Tantra has come to be known as the art of love-making, although it is derived from sophisticated Hindu and Buddhist practices aimed at achieving enlightenment. These practices are rooted in ancient pre-Hindu cultures, which practiced goddess-worship. As sexuality has become increasingly separated from spirituality, the divinity-centered, feminine wisdom enshrined in Tantric practice can supply the precious sexual healing that we all need today.

Divine energy

Western interpretations of Tantra use the techniques of *Kundalini* yoga, breathing and visualization, meditation, dance, and sensual massage to cultivate sensuality in its broadest sense. Traditional Tantric methods include the contemplation of deities (in order to identify with and develop the attributes of the divine in ourselves); colorful and dramatic rituals; sacred art and movement, and subtle yogic practices for transforming worldly passions into rarefied states of bliss and enlightened awareness.

The following techniques describe ways to harmonize the subtle energies of the body, and are the foundation of many rituals included in this book.

Kundalini: the sexual powerhouse

The *Satchakra Nirupana Tantra* discusses five energy-bodies: the physical body, which is described as literally made of food; the energy body, comprised of breath (*prana*); the mental body, which organizes our lived experience into a framework of understanding; our spiritual body, which we develop through meditation, prayer, and ritual practice; and the bliss body. The bliss body is the goal of Tantric practices, because this sense of merging with god can be realized through union with your beloved, as *Shakti–Shiva*. The term Shakti–Shiva refers to this state of bliss as well as to the goddess Shakti and her consort Shiva.

Kundalini energy is known as universal Shakti (goddess) energy. It is thought to lay coiled at the base of the spine, waiting to be awakened by spiritual practice. In Tantric rituals, it is important to raise your energy first, then get it flowing, permeating your body, before relaxing into the state of expanded awareness produced.

Before love-making, or doing any of the exercises in this book, warm up and get your energy moving by dancing, or Kundalini shaking (see page 28). Then move your energy through chakras (energy centres) with help of your breath or visualization (see following page).

The chakra system

Chakra techniques teach us how to invigorate the Kundalini energy-body with the aid of breathing and visualization. Chakra meditations (see page 74) help with emotional de-toxing, purifying the energy-body and deepening our ability to give and receive energy – or love – within any relationship.

Hindu and Buddhist Tantric practitioners describe the energy-body as a series of concentrated wheels of energy, or vortices, where energy spirals abound. There are seven principal chakra points on the body, and hundreds of minor ones, which constitute a network of subtle energy channels, or *nadis*. They believe that stimulating these wheels, or chakras, helps the Kundalini, or energy-body, on its journey from the base of the spine up toward the crown of the head. When this Kundalini energy reaches the crown chakra, or vertex, you will become enlightened, as the

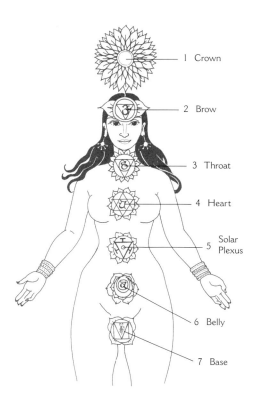

1 Crown

2 Brow

3 Throat

4 Heart

5 Solar Plexus

6 Belly

7 Base

vertex represents the gateway linking your individual energy-body with the energy of the universe. This is considered achievable through the mastery of breathing techniques, yoga postures, and meditations to encourage the Kundalini to rise to the crown chakra. Some adepts, most famously the Buddha, realized enlightenment through their total concentration on this objective.

Breathwork and visualization

Tantric breath is concerned with balancing and uniting the upward and downward movement of breath (which is related to energy and consciousness respectively). To prepare yourself for the breathing exercises in this book, start working every day on the complete breath (see page 10). This is a slow inhalation followed by holding the breath for several seconds (once this length of time becomes comfortable), then a slow exhalation, followed by a pause before the next inhalation.

When you are familiar with this breath, you can begin to visualize the breath flowing in through your lungs and down your central energy channel, which contemporary Tantric teachers such as Margo Anand call the "inner flute". Take the breath right down to the energy source at the base of your spine, and then allow your breath to flow up again, passing through your heart on the way.

Meditation

Meditation focuses attention on the chakra energy centers in the body, mapping out the movement of energies in our bodies to increase awareness and transform consciousness.

The best posture to meditate in is "easy pose", which helps to keep your back upright while sitting for long periods. Sit with your feet crossed at the level of the calves so that each foot is under the opposite knee.

If you want to sit so that you are touching your partner, a good posture is the half-lotus. To get into this posture, sit cross-legged and bring your left foot under your right thigh. Then pick up your right foot with one hand under the right ankle and the other under the shin. While holding it, relax the leg, ensuring that it feels heavy. Then lift it, and bring the heel into the angle of your left groin, with the sole of your foot facing upward. When you are both in this position you can sit closely face to face, with each right knee resting on your partner's left knee. This circulates energy between you, creating a circuit for exchanging energy.

These energy-circuits are known as power forms, or *yantras* (see page 226).

Meditation is fundamental to changing your consciousness. These instructions, adapted from an ancient Tantric text thought to date from the 6th century BC are hard to better:

◆ *Look at an ordinary thing with the consciousness of the god Shiva, as if you are seeing it for the first time.*

◆ *Experience divinity simply by looking steadily at the blue sky beyond the clouds.*

◆ *Wherever your attention lights, experience without attachment.*

◆ *Look at the empty space inside a bowl without focusing on its walls. Absorb yourself in this empty space, which is the nature of existence.*

◆ *Feel yourself emanating in all directions, which is your essential self.*

◆ *Put your attention neither on pleasure nor suffering, but in the place between these.*

◆ *Be absorbed in the sound of a stringed instrument, or a song.*

- *When eating or drinking, become the taste of food and drink, and savor the joy.*
- *To find bliss, enter satisfaction deeply, wherever it is found.*
- *Withdraw your mind from the object of desire and identify with desire itself. This way you become desire.*
- *Eyes closed, see your inner nature as divine.*
- *Meditate on your body as burning into ashes, and become purified.*
- *Place your whole attention on the energy channel, delicate as a lotus stem, in the center of your spinal column. See the lightning like Kundalini successively piercing each center of energy. In this place, be transformed.*
- *Meditate on the Shakti (Kundalini) energy rising from the muladhara chakra (at the base of the spine) like the rays of the sun, getting subtler and subtler until it dissolves into consciousness.*
- *During sexual union, merge into your beloved, and absorb the divine energy.*

Emotional clearing

Before starting on any Tantric ritual, it is important to take responsibility for yourself and your own feelings by clearing negative emotions and centering yourself (see the emotional clearing ritual on page 18). This avoids the transference of negative emotions to your partner that inhibit the vital exchange of energy between you. You can also try the fire-breath ritual (see page 210), a meditation that burns through obstacles to happiness in your partnership.

Many rituals begin with a namaste (see page 2), when you bow to your partner in reverence before working together in sacred space. Through emotional clearing, you can feel truly devotional, rather than resentful, toward your partner; this will empower you both, firing your positive intent toward your relationship.

Making rituals

Cultivating an attitude towards ritual increases your awareness of the sacredness of life. It is this awareness that can help you step beyond self-imposed limits, into closer connection with your partners, and into a much more intense sexual experience. The exercises in this book are not just about novelty or exotic sex; they are about sacred sex. This means that sexual exchange should take place in a ritual atmosphere.

To fully benefit from these rituals, always begin by setting your intent before you begin. Because your energy follows your thoughts, creating a clear intention means that your energy will flow according to your conscious direction. If you're not sure what you're doing or why, your energy will be inhibited or confused. If, however, you are focused and fully aware of your intent, this means you can be in the present and free of distraction, so that the divine energies you're calling upon can move unimpeded through a clear conduit in your mind. Focus on the following:

◆ *Ritual expands sex into a spiritual dimension.*
◆ *Ritual helps us to create the atmosphere we need to do things with a sense of sacredness.*

◆ *Through awareness of the sacred we can step beyond our normal limits, into closer connection with our partners, and into much more intense sexual experience.*

◆ *The most essential aspect of ritual is doing things with awareness. Awareness means being fully present with what you are doing, without your mind wandering.*

By using ritual, you are deliberately making sex sacred, bringing your soul and sex into a potent relationship with one another. Realizing this sacredness in everyday life enables you to celebrate your relationship – and your existence – with joy and love.

1

·•·

HONOR YOUR PARTNER WITH
A NAMASTE

Tantrics believe that in order to experience life as divine, all that is needed is a shift of awareness. You are already divine; you just have to wake up to that fact. You don't need to alter anything or work to improve anything about yourself – you are innately divine. In order to change consciousness, Tantrics use ritual practices to become receptive to divinity.

The *anjala mudra* is a hand gesture used to honor and welcome a deity. This gesture, where the hands are pressed together as if in prayer, is used in the Hindu form of greeting, *namaste*. Use this greeting to express your appreciation of your partner as a unique embodiment of the divine. The divine is another name for boundless love. By acknowledging love as your fundamental reality, you encourage it to manifest.

The aim of this exercise is not to *act* as if you worship your partner, but to open your heart and allow love to flow through you. By bowing to your partner, you treat him or her as the archetypal sacred lover, the Beloved, and so connect deeply, at a soul level. By honoring your lover in this way you may find that you become more observant of your attitude, as this ritual means you automatically step into a heartfelt orientation of love and respect for them. It is good practice to commence each of the night's rituals in this book with a namaste.

If you feel like giggling or making a joke of the whole thing, be aware that this is a form of resistance. The best way to deal with it is to take a moment to register the impulse to laugh and then continue, as you will only gain insight into the potential of the namaste ritual through entering the spirit of this practice.

Ritual

◆ *Start by simply standing facing each other in a relaxed manner. Do this for a few moments until you feel calm and peaceful. Gaze into your partner's eyes. To help maintain visual focus, gaze into each other's left eye.*

◆ *Breathe in, and imagine that you are drawing up your energy through the soles of your feet and into your heart.*

As you do this, bring your palms together in front of your heart, in the gesture of prayer.

◆ *As you breathe out, bend forward slowly so that you bring your foreheads together, still gazing into each other's eyes. Focus your awareness on the meeting of the third eye (in the center of your eyebrows). As you breathe in, draw your awareness back to your heart center. As you breathe out, move back into an upright posture and allow your energy to flow back down toward the earth.*

Variation

While bowing, say aloud,

"I honor you as one of the many faces of the divine."

2

CONSECRATE YOUR RELATIONSHIP THROUGH COMMITMENT

In order to discover the infinite possibilities within an intimate relationship, it is vital to strengthen your commitment to one another. This ritual helps to nourish your relationship on a soul level, and reaffirms the love you have created together. Your relationship is an entity greater than the two of you, and needs to be nurtured.

Voicing your intentions toward each other encourages you to explore the ways in which you can shape your relationship, and enrich it further.

Ritual

Prepare the room with soft candlelight, oil burners, and gentle background music. To create a loving ambience, start this night's exercise with a generous kiss or a whole-body hug, melting into your partner's embrace without restraint. After several minutes' embrace, invite your partner to sit facing you on some comfortable, soft cushions. Share a glass of wine and other refreshments, and offer each other some snacks.

When you are feeling close and comfortable together, use a simple breathing meditation to create a ritual atmosphere. Start by allowing your breathing to fall in time together; take long, deep breaths, allowing your pattern of breathing to slow down simultaneously, so that you are both breathing in and out at the same easy, relaxed pace. This will calm your mood and foster an open connection between you. It is important to establish this warmth and trust before you start to talk.

Next, focus your attention on allowing your love for each other to radiate from your heart center (in the center of your chest) and permeate your whole being. After several breaths, expand these loving feelings to completely envelop your lover. In your mind's eye, visualize the two of you as a couple tenderly wrapped in love.

Make your vows, sipping from the wine goblets with arms entwined.

◆ *Start by affirming your decision to remain together by choice.*

- ◆ *Take turns to describe what you value about your partner, and tell your lover why you are committed to the relationship.*
- ◆ *Talk about the ways you have blossomed, and what you appreciate about the unexpected ways the relationship has unfolded.*
- ◆ *Articulate how you see the fundamental principles in your relationship: whether honesty, fidelity, companionship or adventurousness.*
- ◆ *Share what you would like to improve.*
- ◆ *Outline the aspects that you plan to work on, and what you hope to nurture.*
- ◆ *Listen to your partner express his or her feelings about you and the dynamics of your relationship.*
- ◆ *Hear your partner's intentions for the coming year.*
- ◆ *Reiterate what you value in your relationship, and how it nurtures both of you.*
- ◆ *Express your mutual appreciation and respect for one another.*
- ◆ *Celebrate your desire to give each other pleasure, as well as to access bliss within your self.*
- ◆ *Acknowledge the sacredness of sexuality, and its power to transform your life.*

8

On the first anniversary of our meeting, we created a ritual to celebrate our intention to remain together for the coming year. We covered the bed with red satin and decorated the room with a red silk scarf as a backdrop. I arranged some lovely stones and gems around the room and we prepared an altar with candles and flowers. In the middle of the altar, I arranged two pink roses with a ring on each stem.

After a meal and bath, we anointed our naked bodies with oils and garlanded each other with wild flowers. We spoke our own vows as we exchanged rings. It was so moving that my body was trembling with emotion. It was a loving, beautiful exchange.

3

·◆·

BREATHING MEDITATION

O Radiant one, the experience of awakening may dawn
between two breaths; after it comes downward, before
turning upward. At this moment you can touch your energy-
filled center. When you have exhaled, in that moment's
pause, your sense of small self vanishes and you can realize
the beneficence of existence.

VIJNANA BHAIVARA

 Breath is the source of your vitality, and stimulates
your energy-body. In Sanskrit, the word for "breath"
means "spirit".

Meditation helps you concentrate by focusing your mind
on your essential nature as an energy-body, rather than your
ability to process thoughts. Most meditation practices start

with paying attention to your breath, encouraging mindful presence through focusing your awareness. The simplest technique is to observe the rise and fall of your breath. When you have become absorbed in your own breathing, you can use visualization to facilitate and encourage the natural energy processes that occur in your body.

The aim of this exercise is to learn to breathe fully, right down into your abdomen. It enables you to expand your lung capacity, and slow down the rate of your breathing. These are the first steps to developing more advanced breathing exercises for use in ritual sex. Tantric breath is concerned with balancing and uniting the upward and downward breath, as a means of uniting energy and consciousness.

Ritual

Sit back in a chair with a straight back to allow energy to move freely up and down your spine. If you are alone, rest your hands on your knees, with palms upturned to receive energy. If you are a yoga practitioner, sit in easy pose (*sukhasana*), with your legs loosely crossed one in front of the other.

If you are meditating with your partner, sit cross-legged in front of each other. Rest your left hand on your knee, facing upward, to receive the palm of your partner's right hand, which is facing downward. You can both sit in a half-lotus, dovetailing the postures with each other so that your right knee rests on your partner's left knee (see page xvii).

◆ *Ensure that your body is comfortable and relaxed. Relax the muscles of your neck, shoulders, jaw, mouth, tongue, and forehead, as well as around your eyes.*

◆ *Inhale through your nose, drawing in the breath steadily and gently. Breathe into your abdomen, allowing the breath to fill your abdomen slowly, by letting the chest open without your shoulders rising upward. As you exhale gently, allow your abdomen to naturally hollow.*

◆ *Let any thoughts that enter your mind come and go without captivating your interest. Keep bringing your awareness back to your breathing. Breathe in, hold, and then gently release.*

There are four parts to the traditional yogi breathing known as the complete breath: a slow inhalation followed by holding the breath inside your lungs for several seconds (once this length of time becomes comfortable), then a slow exhalation, followed by a pause before the next inhalation. While holding the breath in, visualize yourself taking in the vitality of the air in your lungs. While breathing out you can imagine that your breath is a fire, which burns up all impurities.

This technique is called the complete breath because the pause is used in meditation to allow your consciousness to expand beyond the process of breathing. Practice the complete breath until it feels easy and natural, starting with only a short pause after inhalation and exhalation. Then lengthen the holding-in stage of your breath, as well as the exhalation, so that you inhale for a count of one, hold for four, and exhale for two.

Variation

As you breathe in, imagine drawing the energy of the breath into the area of your heart.

4

HEART-TO-HEART BREATHING

We faced each other, gazing steadily into each other's eyes.
My breathing became slow and deep, and hers fell into my
rhythm. I noticed that she breathed in my exhalation,
drawing it in gently as if she were savoring its life-giving
properties. I felt as if our breaths were ocean waves, rolling
in and out between us, with each breath. I imagined us lying
on a tropical beach, arms wrapped around each other as the
waves lapped at our bodies.

This meditation exercise strengthens the connection
between your heart and sexuality. The heart is central to the Tantric energy map. It is crucial to open this chakra
of the heart (located between the breasts), allowing loving
energy to flow out of your own body and into that of your

beloved. You can open your heart by harnessing the force of your sexual passion, holding its heat until you burst into ardent flames. The flames from this fire will burn through all the obstacles in your relationship.

When you open your heart and join it with that of your lover, you are both entering the flame of love. Allow the fire of your passionate nature, and the intensity of your experience, to encourage you to love each other without reservation or any holding back.

LOVING MEDITATION

Meditation engenders a deeper connection with yourself and your partner. By sharing a sense of being in the moment – cutting out external distractions – you come closer to one another. Ritual love-making demands you enter a state of meditation during sex, so it's important to be able to create this mood whenever you wish.

Ritual

You may want to use some slow, gentle, romantic music as an accompaniment to the breathing.

Practice the exercise with eyes closed at first. It will help you to pay attention to your internal processes, without immediately trying to synchronize your visualization with your partner.

◆ *Sit with a straight spine and close your eyes. Lay your hands on your chest, over the area of your heart chakra (between your breasts).*

◆ *When you inhale, draw your breath down from your mouth into the area of your heart. Pause at the end of the in-breath, keeping your attention focused on your heart area. Release your breath, and slowly exhale. Continue this heart breath for several minutes.*

◆ *Now open your eyes and gaze at your partner lovingly. Breathe in together, simultaneously drawing the energy of your breath into your own heart center. Pause at the end of the in-breath, focusing on your heart area and allowing the sense of fullness to expand through your chest and throughout your body.*

For several minutes, focus on filling your heart with love. Let love permeate your body with each in-breath. Then, with every out-breath, focus on sending those loving feelings to your partner.

Variation

Visualize your breath flowing in through your lungs and down your central energetic channel, or "inner flute" (see page xvi). Take the breath right down to the energy source at the base of your spine, and then allow your breath to flow up again, passing through your heart on the way.

5

EMOTIONAL CLEARING THROUGH MEDITATION

 Tantra is a spiritual path that relies on opening your heart. As a path of the heart, it celebrates your loving relationship with your beloved. This exercise honors the love you create between you, and uses this love to clear away daily irritations and frustrations as they arise. It helps you let go of self-centered ways of relating to each other in order to open up to the grace of love.

Before starting on any Tantric ritual, it is important to take responsibility for yourself and your own feelings by clearing negative emotions and centering yourself. Anger and resentment will prevent the possibility of rising above the prosaic level of your relationship, or transcending your emotions.

When there are negative feelings between you, you need to release them to prevent physical holding and emotional withholding. Use this exercise any time you are wound up or negative about the relationship, to clear the air before commencing ritual sex.

Ritual

Before starting this exercise, center yourself. Stand with your feet hip-distance apart, knees slightly bent and back straight, to align your spine in order to allow energy to flow easily.

◆ *Close your eyes and take a few minutes to go inside, concentrating on your breathing. Focus on your inhalation and exhalation, and just allow your breathing to be as it is. Observe it. Notice that your breathing calms down and becomes longer and more even.*

◆ *As you inhale, imagine your breath is traveling down to the base of your spine, to your tailbone, or to the bones on which you are sitting. As you exhale, imagine it moving back up your spine to go out through your lungs.*

◆ *Now, open your eyes and bow to your partner, to remind yourself to behave respectfully. Do this whole-heartedly. Your intention is to connect with the core of your partner, whatever the superficial disagreements or woundings you feel you have suffered.*

◆ *Just allow stale emotions and critical thoughts to drop away. Let go of your emotions; whether this is anger, resentment, harsh judgments, or self-protective withdrawal. Let go of your attachment to any past hurts or disappointment. Let go of your need to wound your partner in retaliation for your own wounding. By letting all these negative states drop away it is possible to return to a state of just "being".*

If you can't let go of these emotions through silent meditation, use a more dynamic form. You may want to do a soft belly meditation first (see page 98). Since most disagreement is about emotions (such as frustration) rather than content, use gestures to express your feelings. You can shout and jump about, waving your arms around until the energy has dissipated – or been released as laughter. Emotions are just another form of energy; the idea is to let go of your attachment to the particular emotion you are feeling, and express it in another form. Once you've cleansed yourself of negative attachments, energy can flow unobstructed through your energy-body.

If you have been storing anger and feel the need to shout

and scream, once again use meaningless, made-up words to express your anger. As you shout, imagine that your angry words are flames burning away all the negativity that you have been carrying. You can use the passion of your emotions to burn through any obstructive emotions that are getting in the way of love.

My partner sat beside me while I lay on the floor, watching my abdomen rising and falling with my breath. I could hear her breathing fall into the same pattern as mine, and then she lay down next to me. Feeling her attuned to my breathing was very comforting, and I was able to concentrate on breathing deeply down into the base of my spine. I visualized my breath cleansing the channels in my body, exhaling the negativity I'd accumulated over the years, in the form of discolored air. My breath became slow and even. After several minutes it felt as if my breath was breathing me. My mind began to free-wheel; everything and nothing passed through it.

6

•❖•

RECOGNIZING YOUR RELATIONSHIP AS YOUR TEACHER

 The *Kula Anarva Tantra* describes Tantra as the path of the spiritual hero, who is called a hero because "he is free from passion, pride, affliction, anger, envy, and delusion".

An intimate partnership is the perfect vehicle for your spiritual growth. Rather than take the relationship for granted or lose energy deliberating if it is right for you, accept it as given – and that it's perfect for you right now. The issues that arise in a relationship provide opportunities to learn something about yourself. Your lover is a mirror, who reflects key aspects of yourself for your consideration.

Appreciate the work of relating to your partner; recognize your fundamental similarity and try to create an attitude of respect and loving reverence for each other. This attitude affirms your fundamental connectedness at a soul level. Honor the wisdom of your choice of mate.

Ritual

This exercise encourages you to take responsibility for your feelings rather than blame your partner if they fail to meet your needs. It clears away the petty irritations that can create resentment and blocks to intimacy, fostering greater trust and understanding.

First, both of you spend fifteen minutes writing down the things you appreciate and are irritated by in your partner. Then talk in turn about your observations. Try to spend an equal amount of time on each person's issues.

◆ *Start by naming each quality you see in your partner.*
◆ *Ask your partner to reflect back how this quality manifests in you. Identify and name the issues that challenge and irritate you, with the aim of seeing them from a more transpersonal perspective.*
◆ *Ask your partner to comment on how those issues could be used as a tool for spiritual growth. For instance, your impatience might be teaching you how to become more patient; your neediness might be teaching you how to fulfill your own needs, or to focus on the needs of others rather than yourself.*

◆ *Where the qualities seem to be opposite, think about what you could learn from your partner. Then, ask your partner to feed back to you how they view your issues. Ask them for any support they can offer, in ways that might be beneficial for the relationship.*

◆ *Express your commitment to exploring your own emotional issues, rather than expecting your partner to resolve them.*

◆ *Thank your partner for the ways in which they have helped you deal with emotions and situations so far. Say what you have learned as a result of being together.*

Close this ritual with a short meditation. Focus on feeling compassion for your lover's efforts to improve the ways in which they relate. As you feel the compassion growing in your heart, acknowledge the fact that they are doing the best that they can in their life. Just like you, they are struggling to achieve happiness.

Variation

You may wish to extend this to include a compassion meditation (page 112).

7

BECOMING SOUL MATES

 This ritual awakens the soul in your relationship by linking your two hearts into one living, breathing heart, radiating blissful love and compassion.

According to Tantric philosophy, if we accept bliss as real rather than imaginary, we will truly achieve it. To experience bliss, you need to first recognize your true nature as spiritual and see the divine energy in unconditional love. Before you begin this exercise, focus strongly on accepting your mate, rather than analyzing or criticizing, and so receive love's embrace. Know that love is a perfect vehicle through which you can develop spiritually, expressing your soul in the journey through life.

This exercise is a good prelude to love-making, because in Tantra sexual intercourse is seen as an energetic meeting, a coming together of energy bodies as well as physical bodies. In opening your energy-body to your partner, you embrace each other in a harmonious energy field.

Ritual

◆ *Sit facing each other, cross-legged on cushions, or in a dovetailed half-lotus (see page xvii). Gaze into each other's eyes, and let your breath fall into a gentle, even rhythm together.*

◆ *As you breathe in, draw the breath through your nose, pulling it down your spine into the base of your pelvis, where the tailbone rests. As you continue to breathe, visualize the shape described by your in- and out-breath: with every out-breath, let your breath whoosh out in an arc behind you, streaming outwards from the base of your spine up and over your shoulder, like angels' wings. Imagine that this shape of your exhaled breath makes one half of a heart. Together your breath makes up the two halves of a single living, breathing, beating heart.*

8

KUNDALINI SHAKING

At the start of sexual union remain attentive to the fire in
the beginning, and so continuing, avoid the embers at the
end. When you embrace so that your senses are shaken like
leaves, enter into this shaking.

VIJNANA BHAIRAVA TANTRA

Like a cobra which has cast its coils spiraling conch-like three
times and a half around Shiva,
her mouth laid on that other mouth which leads to bliss,
the enchantress of the world,
slender as a lotus stem,
bright as a lightning flash,
lays sleeping,
breathing softly out and in,

murmuring poems in sweetest meters,

humming like a drunken bee in the petals

of the lotus at the base chakra,

how brightly her light shines.

SATCHAKRA NIRUPANA

The Tantric approach to love-making is to raise your energy by stimulating it before relaxing into it. Before love-making, or doing any of the exercises in this book, warm up and get your energy moving by dancing, or Kundalini shaking. Just as the whole of creation is dancing, you can encourage your energy-body to dance by arousing your Kundalini.

Kundalini is not the same as sexual energy. Kundalini is your personal storehouse of the universal Shakti energy of creation. By stimulating your Kundalini, you can increase your receptivity to sexual energy flowing from your genitals and allowing your chakras, or energy centers to open up one by one. When your sexual energy connects to your heart center you may experience a fine energy streaming through your body, as if every cell is gently vibrating.

The aim of this exercise is to focus on the energy streamings that arise around your pelvis and genitals. It is important to be able to allow energy to move around the pelvis, and to encourage this flow during love-making.

Kundalini shaking is a simple way to enliven your body and wake up the energy in the base of your spine and can also be used before meditation or visualization practices. The feeling of vital energy you get from Kundalini shaking helps you include an awareness of your physical and energy-body in your visualizations. This exercise helps your body open to orgasmic response, along with the butterfly (see page 260).

Ritual

Choose some fast, dynamic music that encourages you to relax and shake your body. Close your eyes. Stand with your spine upright, and arms relaxed by your side. Stand up with your feet a comfortable distance apart, bend your knees slightly to ensure they don't lock up, and start shaking your hips from side to side to loosen your pelvis, and stimulate your energy.

Play with different parts of your body. Shake your pelvis vigorously, letting your behind go wobbly, and shake your shoulders, letting your arms hang freely. Shake your head gently, easing out your neck and jaw. You may want to make a noise, to help free up your jaw and throat.

If you can't feel the trembling spreading from your pelvis into your abdomen, then hold your pose and focus on the sensations building up in your body. Let the trembling gradually climb up your legs and thighs, and into your genitals and pelvis. The trembling may feel very fine, or strong and intense. However it feels, don't try to control the feeling; just try to maintain your pose.

Shake vigorously for several minutes, before letting the wilder movements gradually become smaller, leaving a sensation of energy streaming through your body. Enjoy the sensations, and make sure your body is relaxed when you bring the movements to a rest. Enjoy the stillness that comes in the wake of the dynamic energy sensation created by shaking.

PLAYING THE SUN-MOON GAME

 True liberation comes from devotion. You will find your way to inner freedom by accepting the interplay of desire and service in your relationship. In Tantra, you explore the potential of desire by entering it fully. During the sun–moon game, one partner identifies with desire, the other with service.

This exercise can become a meditation on the nature of desire itself, rather than an opportunity to greedily act out any fantasies you have harbored, or pushing the boundaries of what is acceptable for your partner. By focusing on desire rather than release, you can enter fully into the power of desire. When you do this, you explore what it means to try to satisfy your desire, and so ultimately to detach from all desire.

Ritual

Decide how long the exercise will last, from half an hour to the whole night. Swap roles for the same period of time, either on the same night or consecutive nights. For the agreed duration, one of you will be the active (solar) partner, with explicit permission to express your desires. The solar partner explores their wishes, saying what they want, while the lunar (receptive) partner does all he or she can to fulfill those wishes.

Ask for what you want, and how you would like it to be. Focus on receiving. It may be helpful to give your partner feedback about the way they are sensitive to your wishes.

Likewise, the receptive (lunar) partner contacts their soul's capacity for devotional service. The lunar person tunes in to the needs of their partner, focusing on giving rather than receiving. Don't be compelled to do anything that you don't want to do. However, if your partner asks for something that makes you uncomfortable, try not to become angry or resistant – just say gently that you don't feel that you can fulfill that particular request right now, and ask if there is something else that they would like. The game is not a power struggle; it's an opportunity to whole-heartedly enjoy giving and receiving, without worrying about pleasing each other at the same time.

It's good to share your feelings after this exercise, noting where you felt bold, manipulative, guilty, embarrassed, or any other reactions that you experienced.

"We'll play a simple game. For today, I will serve you, and tomorrow you will serve me. Whatever you wish, I will try to fulfill, if it's possible. Let's start now. Let me know what you want from me."

His eyes twinkled with mischief, but I felt a knot of apprehension in my stomach. How would I be able to take responsibility for everything we did today? Usually, he was my guide. So how should I know what to ask of him? What would he want to do for me, and what did I even want for myself? His simple words had thrown me into a panic. He stood looking at me, smiling, waiting for my inner turmoil to clear for me to begin the game.

Finally, we both dropped into a calm, tranquil feeling, like meditation but without doing anything. Looking intently into

the fire, we started some fire breathing. I said that I wanted
to sit on his lap, so I sat with my legs wrapped around his
back, a shawl draped over both of us. I said that I wanted to
kiss without end. This built up such an erotic charge that
energy waves ran up and down our bodies, and we felt
completely immersed in each other. It was no longer my
desire that he was meeting, but the two of us
merged into desire.

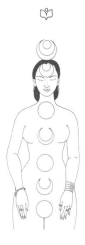

10

•◆•

SEXUALLY PLEASURE YOUR LOVER
FOR AN HOUR (OR MORE)

 This exercise is about learning to say yes to sexual pleasure. It's important to learn to receive in order to let go completely, allowing yourself to fully experience pleasure.

By focusing on one person at a time, you can fully immerse yourself in your own pleasure, without guilt or feeling that you have to reciprocate immediately. This allows you to focus on your own sensations and deepen your erotic sensitivity – and for you to go inside and connect with the subtle movements of energy that occur during sexual arousal. For the partner who's pleasuring you, it's an opportunity to learn what you enjoy and to savor giving sexual pleasure.

In the sun–moon game (see page 32), the lunar (receptive) partner takes responsibility for satisfying their lover's desires. In this ritual, the solar (active) partner takes this responsibility, through giving sexual pleasure. The person being pleasured relaxes into the experience and learns to receive pleasure.

The meditative aspect of the ritual gives you permission to explore your desires by watching them come and go, without getting attached to the outcome. Meditation encourages the personal desires of each partner to emerge from a place of spiritual connection, rather than from personal ego.

Ritual

Take turns to experience aspects of the sun–moon game in giving and receiving pleasure. If you are acting as the solar partner, focus on receiving; if you are the lunar partner, focus on giving sexual pleasure (see page 268).

◆ *Start by meditating together for at least ten minutes. Close your eyes and allow your breath to fall into a slow, steady rhythm, synchronizing with each other's body rhythm. Once you have created a calm, tranquil mood, you can use the radiant energy meditation (page 274) to intensify the meditation.*

◆ *Allow your partner to say what they want, to direct you as to what they enjoy. If they don't know what they enjoy, you can find out by asking to watch while they perform the self-pleasuring ritual (see page 270).*

11
•◆•
CREATE A TEMPLE OF LOVE

 This ritual invites the sacred into your lives through creating a Tantric space, both physically and energetically. Turn your room into a temple of love, and create an altar by placing objects of beauty and inspiration in such a way as to evoke the spirit of the goddess, Shakti, and her consort, Shiva. You can create your own altar to the principles of Shakti and Shiva using objects that invoke their divine qualities. (See pages 178, 182, 194, 240, and 244.)

In creating your altar, you are setting up a sacred space. Before you begin, consider your purpose: to invite the sacred into the bedroom. In ritual, having the right intention is crucial. (Intention just means holding a thought with a particular purpose in mind.) Because your energy follows your thoughts, creating a clear intention means that your energy will flow in the direction that you want it to.

Ritual

Choose a photo of your spiritual teacher, if you have one, or of your beloved, the person you love as your soul mate. Frame it with flowers, and decorate the room with candles and other objects, which have a spiritual resonance for you both. Each object that you bring into the sacred space can have its own meaning and associations for you. For instance, flowers evoke beauty, while water literally is fluidity. Candles, representing fire, are perfect for creating a ritual ambience, as are scents. Choose your favorite essential oil to use in a candle-fired burner. You may like to arrange fresh flowers on the altar – red for the feminine Shakti energy, and white for the male energy of the god Shiva, her consort.

Alternatively, you could choose to represent each of the five elements: a bowl of water with a flower floating on it (water); a crystal or saucer of salt (earth); candles (fire); feather (air); and a stick of incense to remind you of space as you watch the smoke curling upward.

You can "open" your sacred space by beating a gong or sounding a singing bowl, for their vibrant ringing sounds. Tibetan cymbals create a lovely, resonant peal.

12

SEX MAGIC

 Orgasm is an altered state of consciousness, and you can use this moment as a doorway into another dimension of reality. By aligning your sexual energy with the forces of life, you can use its power to harness other forms of energy, literally using sex to make magic.

The most essential aspect of magic is the quality of your awareness. In this exercise, you consciously create an intention to evoke positive forces, and then focus your specific intentions through sacred sex.

Ritual

Discuss with your lover what you most need in your life together. You may wish to consolidate your life as a couple, deepen your relationship, and move forward in your life. You may want to buy a house together or have a child, or integrate your life as a couple within your wider community. If an image comes to mind, you could draw this on paper, to focus your attention on before love-making. You will then find the image in your mind before love-making.

When you are both clear what it is you want, create a circle to represent your ritual space. You can make it out of a garland of flowers, scarves, gemstones, candles, or sand. Sit inside this circle, with the drawing, or a symbol of what it is you want, or with the intention formulated in your minds. Start by bowing to each other (see namaste, page 2).

Next, conjure up in your mind exactly what you want to achieve. If it's about your relationship, imagine the relationship as deeply harmonious, spiritually connected, and lovingly intimate. If it's sexual, imagine that you are both sexually satisfied and radiating fulfillment. If it's Tantric, imagine yourselves as the divine lovers in union, already joined together in a state of bliss.

Whatever your desire is, really imagine yourselves already in that state, using all your senses to bring the visualization alive. Keep this in your mind while love-making. If you have made an image to represent the fulfillment of your desires, look at it, focus on it in your mind's eye during love-making.

Both of you, hold this image or the imagined state in your consciousness as orgasm approaches.

13
•◆•

LIGHTING YOUR SEXUAL FIRE: KUNDALINI MEDITATION

Tantrics visualize the powerhouse of your personal energy as a Kundalini snake, which lies coiled up in the base of the spine, waiting to be awakened and led up through the various energy centers in the body to the crown of the head. Preparation for Tantra involves focusing on this energy and drawing it up through the body in order to create powerful states of spiritual ecstasy.

This fire meditation exercise awakens and stimulates the energy in your root chakra (at the base of your spine), reawakening sexual desire if this has gone to sleep in your relationship. It increases desire, nourishing it as a source of vital energy. When desire is created through meditation, it helps your relationship to become sacred as well as lustful.

Ritual

◆ *Lay down with the soles of your feet touching those of your partner.*

◆ *As you inhale, imagine that you are drawing energy up from your feet, through your legs and into your sexual energy center, in the lower pelvis. In your mind's eye see this breath as a deep, blood red color. At the end of the inhalation hold your breath a moment, allowing the vibrant red light to warm your whole pelvis. As you exhale, encourage this light to expand, saturating your pelvis in its warm red glow. Imagine it expanding so that it invigorates all the cells in your body.*

◆ *Slowly breathe in, hold, and exhale. Each time you breathe in, you are drawing in more warm red energy through the soles of your feet, allowing it to become warmer and hotter, penetrating your whole body to the marrow. Let it radiate, saturating your body with a red glow.*

◆ *As you breathe out, imagine this loving sexual energy expands to include your partner. The energetic effects of this exercise will be enhanced if you are breathing in and out together.*

14

TANTRIC ENERGY MAP: MAP YOUR LOVER'S CHAKRAS WITH HENNA

While playing the sun–moon game I asked if I could adorn my lover's body, marking it with a symbol for our love. With henna paste, I traced a fine floral design, snaking around his lingam like a serpent coiled around a staff, as in the design for the medicinal staff of the Greek god of healing, Asclepius. I chose this motif because the serpent represents the awakening of eroticism in Tantra.

Ritual

HENNA RECIPE

Ingredients:

2 tea bags

2 tsp ground coffee

2 tsp tamarind paste

⅜ pint (15 fl oz) water

2 tbsp sieved henna powder

Cake icing nozzle

5 drops clove or eucalyptus essential oil

If you can't find it ready made, you can make this paste which is suitable for body art. The ingredients should all be available from an Asian shop.

Place the tea bags, coffee and tamarind paste in a saucepan and bring to the boil, then allow to simmer for one hour.

Leave the mixture to cool and add the sieved henna powder, and stir until the mixture is the consistency of icing sugar. Leave the mixture to mature for three or four hours.

Add the clove or eucalyptus oil to the mixture before application. This helps the henna to be absorbed by the skin.

When you have finished your henna design, piping the paste through a cake icing nozzle, leave the henna undisturbed on the skin for as long as possible. The designs should last for up to three weeks. If you don't want to use henna, purchase a skin design pen from a fancy dress store.

In Tantra, the serpent represents the awakening of erotic life energy, known as Kundalini. It moves upward through the body, stimulating the central energy-body, or *sushumna*. The central energy-body starts at the base of the spine, in the area of the tailbone, which forms the first, or base, chakra (see the introduction, page xii). Hindu and Buddhist Tantric practitioners describe chakras as a series of energy wheels, which create the central energy-body. Through mapping your lover's chakras, you heighten your awareness of the points on the body where energy is concentrated.

The most important energy bodies, or channels, are the solar energy channel, which begins in the left ovary or testicle and runs up the right side of the spine, ending at the right nostril; and the lunar channel, which follows a similar trajectory on the left side.

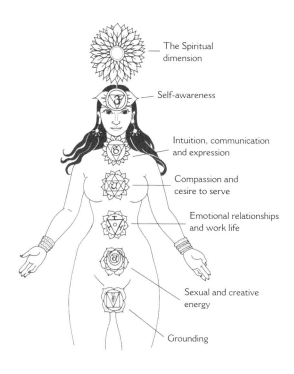

The Spiritual dimension

Self-awareness

Intuition, communication and expression

Compassion and cesire to serve

Emotional relationships and work life

Sexual and creative energy

Grounding

15
.•.

EROTIC TOUCHING

This exercise is intended to help you rediscover the art of sensual touch with your partner – to refine your senses and become completely absorbed in what you are doing. Put your whole awareness into your fingertips and dissolve into your touching. For the receiver, dissolve your whole body in the experience of being touched.

This activity is not necessarily a prelude to lovemaking (although it can be), because it fulfils the desire for sensual touch independent of sex. Create a mood of meditation rather than excitement. Your partner can relax and focus on the experience of receiving, letting go of any expectations or sexual goal.

Ritual

Set the mood with soft, sensual music and invite your partner to lie down naked in a cozy nest made of duvets and cushions. You'll need some long, delicate feathers, such as peacock feathers. Make sure the room is warm.

◆ *Stroke your partner's body gently with a feather, starting around the chest and moving up to the throat. Expand across the shoulders and down the arms, playing with areas such as the inside hollow of the elbow and between the fingers. Then move very slowly and delicately from the area of your partner's heart down their body to the feet, and finish by sweeping up from the heart to the head. Play with curves, hollows, and angles, and include any scarred or damaged areas of skin, giving these areas healing attention.*

Touch feels more exquisite when it is lighter, finer, slower and continuous. So, take your time. Treat every part of your partner's bare skin with loving care and attention, rather than focusing on the usual erogenous zones.

◆ *Then allow your fingertips to barely graze your partner's flesh. Explore the hollows around the shoulders, behind the ears, the inside of the arms and behind the knees. Enjoy your lover's toes. Other areas to explore are the palms and soles of feet, belly, anus, nostrils, the inside of the ear, the edge of little finger, the inside of the thighs, buttocks, and the small of the back and the nipples.*

◆ *Lastly, use your breath to caress your lover's body, blowing about an inch away from the skin (see page 118).*

16

· ◆ ·

ACCESSING SEXUAL ECSTASY

The key to sexual ecstasy is learning to deepen your pleasure. Your physical sensations are a gateway through which to explore your energy-body. Use your feelings of intimacy, trust and relaxation while love-making to develop your erotic potential. Your sexual passion builds up energy that can be channeled into states of rapture. Using meditation and visualization techniques during love-making helps you fully enter your bodily experience.

Ritual

Explore these suggestions; they will encourage you to open even more to sensual pleasure:

◆ *As your lover strokes your face and hair, receive his or her loving touch.*
◆ *When your lover's hands gently caress your flesh, melt into that refined sensation.*

- *When your lover kisses you all over, really feel their loving intent.*
- *Connect with the heart center of your partner, through exchanging breath, or visualization (see page 14).*
- *As your lover embraces you, feel held in a warm cocoon of love.*
- *Inhale the sweet breath of your lover, nourishing your own vitality.*
- *When aroused, focus on your breathing; remain still, breathing slowly and deeply to deepen your arousal.*
- *As your lover plays with your genitals, encourage the erotic fire to build in your pelvis.*
- *As your excitement mounts, focus on drawing your energy from your genitals up your spine (through the central energy channel) into your heart chakra, and then up into your brow (see page 162).*
- *As your genitals come together, allow your sexual pleasure to pervade your heart, where it creates joy.*
- *During love-making, draw the sexual energy from your heart upward into the energy center at the crown of your head, where it creates bliss.*

17

•◆•

FIRE MEDITATION

In the fire offering, man himself becomes the fire. He is the
fuel. His smoke is the smoke, his embers the embers, the
sparks are his sparks. In that fire the gods offer man, and man
rises up shining.

BRHADARANYAKA UPANISHAD

This active meditation uses the image of fire to burn
away any obstacles in your energy-body. Fire has
long been used by Tantrics to burn away all impurities and
obstructions on the spiritual path. By meditating on your
body burning into ashes, you prepare yourself for spiritual
transformation.

This symbolizes the sacrifice of your self. In spiritual
terms, this means your personality, your ego, and your

attachment to your physical body as well as your particular way of looking at reality. You can offer any negative states you wish to transform, such as loneliness, envy, greed, or the need to control, to be consumed by the fire.

Ritual

Use exciting music with a strong beat to help you get into the dynamic mood of this ritual. Read this meditation slowly to your lover, or tape it for both of you.

◆ *Stand with a straight spine and your feet planted on the floor, in alignment with your shoulders. Imagine you are sending roots down into the earth, through your feet. Draw up the energy into your pelvis – the energy of the red fiery flame. Imagine this flame is licking up into your pelvis burning away any sexual blocks. Imagine this fiery red flame is consuming your legs and your pelvis. Imagine you are becoming the fire, the flame. Allow yourself to move and dance as the flame. You become pure energy.*

◆ *As the flame climbs higher, it consumes your pelvis, burning away any creative blocks and firing your creative energy. Let this process express itself in your dance.*

Imagine this purifying flame climbing up to your solar plexus, its voracious tongues of flame clearing the problems in your personality that get in the way of relating to others. Imagine the flames nourishing your sense of empowerment.

◆ *As more and more of your body is consumed, imagine the flame licking the inside of your chest, burning away any grief or emotional wounds in your heart. Then let the fire burn away blocks to self-expression, as it purifies the area of your throat.*

◆ *Let the flames rise to your third eye area in the center of your forehead, consuming redundant ways of viewing the world and others, and cleansing your vision.*

◆ *Imagine the flames rising up through the crown of your head, gradually becoming white. Allow yourself to dance as the flame reaches from your passion into the realm of spirit. Open yourself to the universe.*

◆ *After some time, allow the white-hot flames to recede, leaving you cleansed. Draw the healing white light downward through each chakra.*

◆ *As it subsides into the area of the third eye, it leaves a sense of greater space, vision and clarity.*

- As it comes down through your throat, imagine it enables you to express yourself on every level, strengthening your ability to communicate clearly and effectively.
- As the flame subsides through your heart, feel a great openness.
- In the solar plexus, experience the brilliance of your being and luxuriate in the quality of centeredness that this brings.
- As the red flame flickers around your navel, imagine your sexuality cleansed and renewed. Visualize bright red tongues of flame licking the base of your spine, regenerating your energy and passion for life.

18

THE LOVE MUSCLE

 The love muscle is crucial to improving sexual pleasure. And like any other muscle, it needs to be exercised to become stronger. You will be using this muscle in several exercises to develop more control over your erotic pleasure (see pages 60, 234, and 320) and in love-making to build arousal, increase pleasure, control your orgasm, or extend it. Through developing control over your love muscle you can learn to stimulate and then contain sexual excitement, and release it in orgasm, at will.

The love muscle, or muscles, are known as the PC, or pubococcygeal, muscles. This band of muscles lays across the floor of your pelvis. In Tantra it is called the love muscle, or fire muscle, because it can be used either to intensify or disperse sexual excitement and pleasure. Building strong love muscles will give you control over your sexual fire.

If you have difficulties achieving orgasm, this exercise is very important to improve up your capacity to do so. While Tantric sex isn't about striving for orgasm, your energy cannot be harmonized and exchanged if one partner is regularly reaching a climax while the other is not. It is important for both of you that your excitement and pleasure can repeatedly climb and fall, being released in orgasmic pleasure during love-making.

You can use the breathing exercises in this book (see pages 14, 308, 312 and 352) to increase your orgasmic response by squeezing the love muscle on every in-breath, in order to build up an energy charge. This will intensify the movement of erotic energy produced by the combination of breath and visualization. If you can't feel your love muscle very easily, or it seems weak, you'll need to practice doing at least 100 squeezes a day, varying the speed. These are the same muscles that stop and start your flow of urine. You can practice squeezing and strengthening them anywhere.

Ritual

Begin by sitting upright in a comfortable position, and breathe in a relaxed, even way.

◆ *Breathe in, allowing your lower abdomen to move out as your lungs expand. Relax your whole body as you breathe* out, especially round your hips and lower back. Experience a sense of space in your pelvis. Now, as you breathe in, squeeze your love muscles. Hold your breath for several seconds, and hold the love muscles without tensing the rest of your body. As you breathe out, relax them. Keep breathing in and out, squeezing and relaxing your love muscles, for at least twenty minutes.

◆ To complete the exercise, deeply relax your pelvic organs. As you breathe out, relax your love muscles, and breathe in again without contracting it. On the next out-breath, relax the muscles around your genitals and anus even more. You'll notice that even when you think you're relaxed, you could still let go even more. Notice whether your muscles are still holding any tension, and breathe in and out again, sending your breath to these tension areas to help the muscles release when you next exhale.

◆ Continue to breathe like this for several minutes, encouraging your pelvis, hips, and buttocks to relax. Allow this deep release to permeate your whole body.

◆ Experiment with squeezing your love muscles as you breathe out and relaxing as you breathe in, noticing the difference with the change in your breathing pattern.

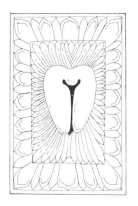

19

FIRE MEDITATION WITH LOVE MUSCLE SQUEEZE

 This Tantric exercise charges up your energy-body by increasing sexual control over the mounting fire of your desire. You can use this technique to build erotic excitement whenever you would like to increase your libido.

The aim of this meditation is to extend the fire meditation you have already done (see page 52), and include the love muscle squeeze (see page 56). As you imagine energy being drawn up through the energy channels of your body, you visualize the flame in each chakra for several breaths, co-ordinating the love muscle squeeze with each breath. The love muscle squeeze seals energy in your body, which increases your erotic desire and pleasure.

Ritual

◆ *Lie on the floor with your knees raised. Lift your pelvis and start rolling it up and down and shaking it to free up* your lower back and abdomen. Keep breathing slowly and evenly as you feel an energy charge build in your pelvis.

◆ Then lie with your back on the floor until your breathing becomes even. Then squeeze the love muscle in time with your breath. Squeeze the muscles around your genitals and anus as you breathe in, and release them as you breathe out.

◆ Imagine a fiery red flame igniting at the base of your spine, around your perineum. Draw the red fiery energy of the flame into your base chakra (see page 47), and allow it to subside on each exhalation. Squeeze the love muscle with each inhalation.

◆ Visualize a raw, red flame in your pelvis. On your in-breath, draw this flame up to your second chakra. Use your hand to trace the path of this flame from your genitals to your navel. As you stroke upward, breathe in and squeeze the love muscle. Release it as you breathe out and, with your hand, follow the energy, returning back to the base chakra.

◆ After a few breaths draw up the red flame into the second chakra, at the navel, with your breath and hand as before, stoking the source of your sexual fire. Clench your love muscle to fan the heat of your desire.

- *As you exhale, relax the love muscle and trace the withdrawing flame back down to your base chakra with your hand.*
- *Next, draw up the flame to the third chakra, above the navel. Do this by breathing these flames first into your navel, then expand the heat into your solar plexus.*
- *Imagine the flame entering your heart. Encourage the flame to climb, squeezing your love muscle as you inhale, gradually relaxing it as you exhale. Bring your hand up to your chest and hold the flame in your heart, as you continue to pump energy into the heart region with your love muscle.*
- *Visualize flames climbing up to your throat chakra. Help them climb with your hand and your love muscle, then let the flames consume your third eye chakra and lick around the crown of your head.*
- *To finish, bring down the flames through each chakra, returning to the base of your spine.*

20

•◆•

DESCRIBE YOUR LOVE-MAKING

 This ritual helps you improve your communication simply through becoming much more verbal about sex. Describing your experience means that your lover will understand what runs through your mind while love-making, and discover more about how you experience sex – what arouses you, and what fails to excite. Your sexual communication will open up, because of the trust involved in sharing at this level of detail.

You can also become aware of your internal commentary during love-making. Many of the thoughts we have during sex distance us from our own experience and are not helpful. Once you understand it, you can make a conscious decision about where your attention is focused. In Tantric terms, concentrating your attention on your energy processes stops you getting distracted by your mind. Start by connecting with each other with heart-to-heart breathing (see page 14) or the heart visualization on page 26.

Ritual

During love-making, each of you describes your feelings, sensations, and emotions as they arise. You can do this together, or take turns during consecutive love-making sessions. Communicate your experience without reservation; express it as an unexpurgated stream of consciousness. In this way, you can guide your partner through your love-making experience openly.

Variation

Self-pleasure your pearl (clitoris) or lingam (penis) for half an hour or so. Describe your experiences, then let your partner take over, while you tell him or her what feels good and what you would like. Try different strokes and rhythms in great detail without having any goal.

21

◆

BODY AWARENESS

Training in Tantra techniques involves developing your powers of concentration in conjunction with increased bodily sensitivity. In exercising your imagination and your ability to retain visual impressions, you can use these faculties to potentize your relationship. This is how you use a yantra (see page 226) – by focusing on a mental image, you direct your energy in a specific way. In this exercise, every action is performed with conscious intent. The words uttered are pared down to a minimum, so that they become ritualistic.

This exercise uses the power of concentration to focus the mind through gazing at your partner. This is important, as it keeps your mental faculties harmonized with your sexual ones. It trains you to keep your whole attention focused on what you are doing with your partner during love-making. Using mind imagery will intensify the experience in a striking way.

Ritual

Begin by taking a glass of wine together, as if sharing a toast.

◆ *Start the ritual with a kiss. Shiva, (the man) says, "I am ready," to announce the beginning of the ritual. At his words, start by slowly undressing him, really looking at each part of his body as you uncover it. Don't ask for his help, and don't touch him more than you need to in order to unclothe him. Disrobe him tenderly, savoring each area as it is revealed.*

◆ *Once you have undressed him, drink in his whole body through your eyes. When you feel you have internalized these impressions, it is your turn to announce, "I am ready," and stand motionless while your lover disrobes you. In his turn, he examines your body with great care and attention.*

◆ *After several minutes of looking, he lifts his arm and gently touches your lips, your nipples, abdomen, and pubic mound, bringing his cupped hands to rest on your vulva. Again, in the act of touching, all his attention is focused on the parts he is touching. If any mental chatter distracts him, he can hum gently to help himself concentrate. Then*

he closes his eyes and, based on these sensory impressions, he spends a few minutes recalling the parts of your body that he has just looked at, in order to build up a composite picture of your whole body.

◆ *Then, take his hands and guide them over your body, touching his fingertips to the same areas he has just touched, while he focuses on keeping the image of your body in his inner eye. Finish by holding his hands cupped over your pubic area. Once you release his hands, he may open his eyes.*

◆ *Now it is your turn to gaze at his body, really taking it in bit by bit. Concentrate on absorbing the impression of his body as you touch his lips, nipples, belly, and penis with the tip of your thumb and first finger. Close your own eyes and evoke his image in your inner eye. Then he will guide your hands over his body, just as you have done to him.*

◆ *Then move into a seated posture together. The woman sits cross-legged, and the man has his knees bent to clasp her waist, with his legs behind his partner's buttocks. Gaze at each other's faces, then the nipples, navel, and finally the genitals. After gazing at your partner's sex for some minutes, close your eyes and visualize their genitals. The*

68

woman imagines her lover's penis becoming aroused, growing and becoming erect, stimulating her clitoris and entering her vagina. The man imagines your vagina becoming moist and juicy, opening and receiving his lingam (penis).

After these visualization exercises you can go on to make love if you wish. Close your eyes during love-making, and continue to recall these internalized images of your lover's body. That way, your mind is always concentrated on your partner's body during sex.

22

•◆•

MAKE LOVE FROM YOUR CHAKRA AWARENESS

 SkyDancing Tantra teacher John Hawken believes your experience of making love depends upon the condition of your chakras. Making love to a woman with your energy concentrated at the level of the first three chakras (base, sexual, and solar plexus) is about ego and personal power, rather than love and connection. Once you have purified the next chakra, the heart center, you can begin to open your heart to deeper love. By surrendering to love, you purify the other chakras: the throat, brow, and crown.

The three most important chakras for awakening the Kundalini – your personal storehouse of universal sexual energy – are the root center at the base of the spine, the heart center, and your third eye chakra, between your eyebrows.

Kundalini energy takes on the different qualities of each chakra as it passes through them. Tantric teachers believe that different levels of relationship are activated according to the degree that you have evolved. The primal instinctual level corresponds to your root chakra, while the sensual level correlates with your belly. Personality and psychological issues are more important at the level of the solar plexus, and your romantic connection corresponds to the heart chakra, the center of love. The chakras above this are activated during intuitive and mystical states of connection. In the brow your relationship is idealistic, often harnessed to your joint orientation toward service on behalf of others. On the crown level (the top of the head), you merge together on a soul level: true soul mates.

This exercise involves consciously exploring the different levels of your relationship and acting them out. If you are making love with the awareness of your base chakra, you'll be connected with your partner at an instinctual level. If you make love from your heart center, you'll be in a state of loving connectedness. If you make love with the awareness of your third eye, you'll be sharing a spiritual vision with your lover. This means you can choose to incorporate these elements in future love-making. Your relationship can evolve as your personal power develops and integrates through opening your chakras.

Ritual

When you make love, choose one of the chakras and focus your energy in that center. Start with a meditation that evokes the qualities associated with that chakra.

◆ *Meditate on the root chakra. Here, you could evoke the instinctual survival qualities of an animal. Choose an animal you identify with and, before you start, imagine you have become that animal. Feel its healthy vitality and absorb its energy as a sense of wellbeing. Make love with your energy located in that center.*

◆ *When meditating on the sexual center, you might identify with different aspects of your sexuality; hedonism, coyness, sensitivity, tenderness, strength, passivity, perseverance, adventurousness. Relate to your sexual emotions with passion.*

◆ *On the level of the solar plexus you might choose to explore a predominant emotion, such as anger, jealousy, shyness, dependency. This center relates to personal power and identifying with it might involve exploring any problematic power issues between you.*

72

◆ *At your heart chakra, you may uncover loving qualities of tenderness, affection, caring and nurturing, and fidelity. Or you may identify with longing, or a spiritual yearning for the beloved. To explore this, make love with a sense of yearning, or of emotional completion.*

◆ *On the throat chakra, you may identify with the need to communicate, or, conversely, the ease of communicating your love and sexual desire. Make love using visualizations as a means of strengthening your awareness. This chakra is about self-expression, so access the mysterious and intuitive aspects of your relationship and try to express them verbally in your love-making. You can also use singing or humming to tune in to this chakra (see page 86).*

◆ *On the level of the brow, you may feel attracted to a vision of an egalitarian relationship, or exploring your idealism. You may wish to hold this vision in mind during love-making (see sex magic, page 40).*

◆ *On the crown level, you may wish to explore a spiritual connection. Make divine love as a god and goddess.*

23

PURIFYING YOUR CHAKRAS WITH
COLOR HEALING

 This meditation exercise purifies the energy-body by using color visualizations for each chakra, or energy center. It will help your relationship if you are finding it diffi-cult to maintain the love between you. Purifying the chakras helps you open your heart, fostering a deeper sense of con-nection with your partner and your own spirituality.

Your relationship is a process rather than a steady state. It exists in the present – not in past experiences or future dreams. Clearing away emotional debris will create clarity and return you to your natural state of aliveness. The ground of your being is aliveness, and an intensity of experience that doesn't have to be strived for. If you clear away old wounds, you will find your passion.

Chakra colors and their healing associations

Chakra	Color	Healing Association
Root (base of spine)	Red	Balancing and grounding
Sexual (genitals)	Orange	Revitalizes your passion
Solar plexus	Yellow	Expands your sense of self and helps you become more dynamic in the world
Heart	Green	Nourishes love and compassion
Throat	Blue	Stimulates your unique creativity, helping you express your inner truth
Brow (third eye)	Violet	Bridges the mind and psyche, helps you access true wisdom
Crown (top of head)	White	Nourishes your sense of connection with the divine, aligning you with love

Ritual

Lie on the floor with your knees raised, or sit on a chair with your feet on the ground. Alternatively, sit in a yoga posture known as the tailor position, with your knees bent out to the sides and the soles of your feet touching. Whichever position you choose, keep your back straight (although not stiff) while doing this visualization.

◆ *Imagine a fiery red light appearing at the base of your spine, around your perineum. Visualize it nourishing your health and vitality.*

◆ *On the in-breath, draw up this light up to your second chakra. Imagine it turning orange as you draw it up into the second chakra, in the pelvis, stoking the fire of your sexuality. Visualize it as an orange light stimulating your passion.*

◆ *Next, as you draw the light up to the third chakra, imagine it turning a vibrant yellow.*

Breathe this yellow light into your navel, expanding out into your solar plexus, nourishing your sense of emotional wellbeing.

- *Imagine the light turning green as it enters your heart, filling you with love and compassion.*

- *Then imagine blue light pouring into your throat center, strengthening your intuition.*

- *The light becomes violet as it reaches your third eye chakra, stimulating your self-awareness and visionary capacities.*

- *Imagine the light becoming white as it plays around the crown of your head, filling you with a sense of spiritual connectedness.*

- *Draw the pure white light down through each chakra, cleansing each one in turn as it descends toward the base of the spine.*

24

•◆•

RECITE A MANTRA:
WORDS OF POWER

Intone the a-u-m slowly, which is the sound of existence.

VIJNANA BHAIVARA

 A mantra, or invocation is literally a "tool to thought". Sacred sounds are recited to align oneself with the divine. The famous seed-syllable, Om, is considered to be the sound of the universe vibrating. In Sanskrit, Aum, or Om, is a power word that represents the spiritual reality behind our manifest physical world. Hindus believe it is sacred, because it expresses the essential spiritual nature of the universe.

Chanting focuses your mind, allowing you to cut through mental busyness to deeper states of awareness. Just as sacred images provide a focal point for concentration, power words act as magnets to attract subtle vibration. Specific sacred syllables have acquired spiritual resonance through daily recitations over thousands of years.

Seed-syllables and the chakras

You can tune the chakras by intoning the seed-syllables for each chakra:

Seed-syllable	Chakra	Healing benefit
LAM	Root	Grounding
VAM	Sexual	Building sexual energy
RAM	Solar plexus	Regulating emotional relationships and work life
YAM	Heart	Developing compassion and the desire to serve
HAM	Throat	Accessing intuition, communication, and expression
AUM	Brow	Expanding self-awareness

Ritual

Intone the seed-syllable Aum (Om) to mark the beginning and end of your time together in ritual space. Together, chant it at the open and close of the ritual. This is the sound of the creative energy of the universe, and reciting it helps to harmonize you with cosmic energy.

Chant A-u-m in three equal parts.

◆ *Let the sound arise from your belly. Chant "Ah", where the sound springs from your navel.*
◆ *Chant "Oh", allowing the sound to pour out of your chest from your sternum.*
◆ *Chant "Mm", where the sound reverberates in the throat center.*
◆ *Allow the sound to vibrate through your whole body, allowing all the tissues to reverberate with this sacred sound, until you become a tuning fork resonating with the energy of the cosmos.*

When you become familiar with intoning Aum, you can add this visualization:

- *As you chant "Ah", see a lotus in your pelvis, which represents life itself. The petals shimmer bright red.*
- *As you chant "Oh" from your heart center, see the iridescent red petals become a translucent pink, with a pink heart.*
- *As you chant "Mm" from your throat center, see the tips of the lotus become a luminous white, with a pink heart.*
- *Allow yourself to merge with this lotus flower, becoming one.*

He began to hum what sounded like Om. The sound filled my chest and warmed my heart. I played with intoning Om until I felt a deep stillness and unity. Love was growing in my heart, and I closed my eyes to savor our connection. We hummed together for several minutes, until the sound fell back into the rolling waves of our mingled breath. I surrendered to the flow of breath between us, and through this I felt a sense of deep union with him.

25

SINGING THE PRAISES OF THE GOD
AND THE GODDESS

 Singing is a form of mantra (see page 78) – a way of using power words. In singing praises to deities, you identify and incorporate the god and goddess into your self. To realize that the nature of existence is divine – that is, love – means recognizing the all-embracing god and goddess within yourself and your love partner. Women are manifestations of the goddess, Shakti, and men of the god, Shiva. When you unite with your partner in love, you integrate yourself with your other half, becoming whole.

This exercise attunes you to the spiritual vibrations of the universe. As a regular practice, it calibrates your energy-body to the same resonance as the deity you invoke. Singing provides a gateway for the energy of the deity to enter your own consciousness, helping you incorporate divine qualities or energies in your life.

Ritual

To worship the feminine principle, you can sit in front of a symbol of the yoni (female genitalia), such as a conch shell, or a statue of a goddess using red roses as an offering. Say something like: "with these red flowers, I invoke the qualities of love, passion and compassion. I call these qualities to me."

You can then chant the following mantra, which is a play on the syllables making up the goddess Tara's name. It starts with Aum (Om), the sound from which all things are created (see page 78). Tara is the goddess who represents loving compassion. If it helps you focus your chanting visually, sit in front of an image of Tara, and feel the loving compassion associated with her radiating from your heart center, between your breasts, as you sing her mantra:

Aum Tara

Aum Ta-ra Tut-ta-re Tu-re So-ha

Aum Ta-ra Tut-ta-re Tu-re So-ha

If you would prefer to try a mantra that comes from the Christian tradition, the writer Swami Sivananda Radha suggests chanting to the rhythm of Ave Maria:

> Most beautiful Mother my heart is on fire
> To love thee and serve thee is all I desire
> Av-e Av-e Av-e Ma-ri-a.
> Av-e Av-e Ma-ri-a

TO SHIVA

Shiva is the Hindu god whose primal dance is responsible for bringing the created world into being. Sit in front of an image of Shiva, the representation of masculine energy and consciousness, or any object that reminds you of a phallus. To accentuate the ritual ambience before chanting, you can lay white flowers in front of his image. Say something like, "with these flowers I invoke the qualities of conscious awareness, clarity and focus. I call these qualities to me." Then chant:

> Aum Na-mah Shi-va-ya
> Aum Na-mah Shi-va-ya
> Aum Na-mah Shi-va

·•·

26

VOICE MEDITATION DURING ORGASM

Intone a sound aloud, then less and less audibly as the sound
deepens into a silent harmony.

VIJNANA BHAIVARA

Harnessing the power of your throat chakra (see
page 74) helps you express your full sexual potential.
When your throat chakras are harmonized during love-making, your sexual creativity and expression is nourished, and a
deeper sexual intimacy is encouraged.

Vocalizing during sex expands the experience for you in
other ways, in regulating and balancing aspects of your
metabolism. The throat center is connected with sound and
hearing (hence the use of mantras): speech and silence, inhaling and exhaling, and the divine metabolism of the god Shiva
and goddess, Shakti.

Ritual

◆ *Start the ritual with your lover arousing your body (see pages 240–55 and 268).*

◆ *As your partner stimulates your genitals, imagine that sexual energy is spreading down your legs and up into your chest. Imagine that the energies aroused by your sexual excitement are flowing from your sexual center up to your heart. Both of you, focus on expanding your loving feelings as well as enjoying your genital pleasure as you become more sexually aroused.*

◆ *As it collects in your heart, send this energy back to your lover as an outpouring of loving kindness. Imagine your partner cocooned in the warmth of your love.*

◆ *As orgasm starts, breathe in deeply and slowly, and as you breathe out make as much noise as you can, because the volume of your sound can influence the volume of your orgasm. Use whatever sounds you are comfortable with, or try a long, slow "Ah". Try to keep vocalizing for several long breaths. Vocalizing also opens your throat center, helping pull energy upward through the chakra system. You can facilitate it by imagining pulling the golden sexual energy up with your breath, first into your heart, and then*

your throat center. Once you have managed to visualize your breath coming up through these successive chakras, you can imagine your breath as golden light pouring out your throat as you vocalize in whatever way you want.

Variation

Experiment with reciting a mantra (page 78) to open out the throat center, the chakra associated by Tantric practitioners with communication, expression, and intuition.

◆ *During slow and gentle intercourse, develop a slow rhythm that allows you to focus on your breathing. Allow the rate of your breath to fall in time together. After several minutes of synchronized breathing, intone the sacred sound Aum (Om) with each exhalation, directing the sound to the heart center of your lover. Your lover returns the sacred sound to your heart, by chanting Aum with every out-breath.*

◆ *As the contractions of your orgasm start, breathe in deeply and slowly, and as you breathe out make as much noise as you can – hum if you feel embarrassed. Vocalizing helps prolong your orgasm, and it opens your throat*

chakra, helping to pull the sexual energy released at orgasm up the energy channel along your spine. Tantra teacher Margot Anand calls this conduit the "inner flute" (see page xvi).

27

•◆•

GAZE INTO YOUR LOVER'S SOUL

His dark curls kissed his cheeks, just as I wanted to. I savored
him as I tongued my wine glass, chalice of Aphrodite.

I closed my eyes and sank into the background, chanting. It
was a hymn to the gods. I didn't know what it meant, but
when I opened my eyes I thought, "This sublime man is
definitely my god. Soft curls kissing a face that's almost too
beautiful to look at, dark eyes that would scare me if they
weren't wavering themselves." My fingers traced his
cheekbones, gently brushing his lashes before wiping away
the querulousness and ambivalence on his succulent features.
He held me in his regard. I liked to feel held, and I liked to
feel I could hold him. I relaxed into his gaze. It felt familiar,
easy, encompassing.

In Eastern cultures, looking is regarded as active. By gazing, you in some way possess the thing you look at. In energy terms, you absorb part of what you behold, and you offer yourself up to the beholder. So, looking is an energy exchange and the eyes a potent medium for this exchange.

You can use this potent sense to deepen your connection with your lover. Look at him or her in order to reach into their true nature. Let this be your meditation; gazing into the soul of your beloved, through the gateway of their eyes.

Ritual

For this ritual it is important to hold your gaze steadily. Put all your awareness into your gaze; just looking without paying attention to the mind and its running commentary. If your mind is restless, focus your inner eye on this visualization. Close your eyes and bring your partner's face into your mind's eye. Paint their face as you recall all the details of their skin, eyes, mouth and expression. Let this image rest awhile in your mind, before slowly opening your eyes.

You can do this exercise naked, or wearing a few transparent robes.

- *Sit a couple of feet across from your partner and close your eyes. Focus your awareness inside. Gaze at your beloved. Open your eyes to their divine nature. Your partner is truly a god/dess. Drink in the beauty of their form. Let your eyes travel over their soft warm flesh, delighting in the curves and planes of their body.*

- *Once you have drunk in their contours, bring your eyes to rest on your partner's face. Spend several minutes looking, before holding your lover's gaze, unblinking, for the longest moment. Relax into the looking, until you feel you become the looking. Carry on for several minutes longer, entering into their eyes, glimpsing the soul.*

- *Look into your partner with a gaze full of love. Let your love flow out through your eyes, warming your beloved's heart. Anoint their body with your eyes.*

If it is difficult for you to sit quietly and just look at your partner, start with ten minutes, gradually increasing the time. You don't need to say anything; speaking will break your concentration.

If you need to stop your eyes switching from one eye to another, direct your gaze into your partner's left eye. In

Tantra the left eye is associated with lunar, receptive energy, while the right eye is associated with active solar energy.

Variation
You can do this gazing meditation to keep your lover in your mind's eye when you are apart.

◆ *Look at an image of your lover. Imbue it with the healing balm of your love.*
◆ *Once it is charged with the power of your love, place this image of your lover in your heart center. Imagine your lover sitting within your heart, wrapped in love.*

I asked him to gaze at a photo of me every day: a daily practice to melt his heart, which was armored against grief.

28

⚬•＋•⚬

DEMON DIALOGUE

 When you notice obstacles in your sexual relationship, blocks to your sexual pleasure, or resistance coming up when you try the exercises in this book, these are signs that your body is holding back and your energy-body sluggish. Holding may feel like armoring, which stops you feeling your sensations properly. It may feel like withholding, keeping you from developing deeper intimacy and reducing your sensitivity, both emotionally and sexually. Toxic emotions may make you afraid or timid, or guilty or ashamed, depending on the past experiences you hold in your body-memories. Externalizing them as "demons" helps to remove their hold on your vitality and sexuality.

You can use this exercise to access held emotions, converting them into imaginary monsters to grapple with, in order to transform them into constructive energy. Once you know what you are dealing with, you can engage with your imaginary demons and enter into a dialogue with them.

Ritual

◆ *Place two cushions facing each other, and sit on one of them. Your partner will sit to the side to act as your witness and provide whatever support you need.*

◆ *Close your eyes and go inside to invoke your demon. Focus on the fear, anger, numbness, or resistance you experience in your sexual relationship. Do this by sensing the energy of the emotion. Locate it in your body. Where do you feel it? What does it look like, feel like, how does it smell? Breathe into it. In your mind's eye, give it life.*

◆ *Visualize this energy as a demon – its shape, form, posture, movements, and sound. As you see the demon emerging, become it. Mimic it by assuming its posture and adopting its sounds and movements. Exaggerate its movements in order to discover what it feels like to have this demon possessing you.*

◆ *Once you have evoked this demon, get it out of your body. Direct its energy onto the cushion in front of you and feel it as pure energy. This monster is just another form of energy that you can now observe. As you sit on your own cushion, feel the quality of the energy emanating from this demon. What is it like to live under the grip of this demon?*

◆ *To separate yourself from the demon, confront it and ask why it is trying to punish you in this way. Say out loud exactly how you think it is controlling or limiting you.*

◆ *When the ways in which the demon controls you have become clear, visualize a scepter of light in front of you. It is upright, parallel to your spine, and the handle is at the level of your heart. In your imagination, reach out and take hold of the scepter in order to connect it with your own heart and your consciousness.*

◆ *Call on your own inner intention and shine the light of the scepter on the demon. Holding it like an amulet, ask "What do you really want?"*

◆ *Swap cushions and sit in the place of the demon. Reach into your unconscious, and in the light of consciousness answer the question about what you want. Articulate this, so that your witness can hear what you have to say.*

◆ *Once you have understood what the demon requires of you, move back onto your own cushion. Spend a few moments thinking about how you can accommodate the needs of the demon to prevent it taking possession of you once again. Then turn to your partner and describe the*

internal process you have been through. Ask your partner to share what they have observed.

◆ *Together, talk about ways in which you can transform this demon in your relationship.*

29
·•◆·

SOFT BELLY MEDITATION

 Your belly is the center of your personal power. The state of your solar plexus, in the upper belly, reflects the health of your sense of personal power, while your lower belly reflects your sexual energy.

Holding emotions in the area of your belly will block the flow of energy through your body, producing emotional and sexual disharmony. When your belly is hard and armored as a result of anger or fear, it prevents your body responding to the fire of your sexual passion, which also blocks the connection between your sexuality and your heart.

To prepare yourself for this exercise, your lover massages your abdomen. This relaxes and releases the muscles, softening your body and the source of your erotic energy, and preparing you to open up on more subtle levels.

Ritual

◆ *With one hand on each side, stroke the area just under the rib cage, starting in the center and tracing the curves out to the side of the body. Use long, sweeping strokes with some pressure, without causing discomfort.*

◆ *Then use similar long, sweeping strokes from the middle of the diaphragm (where the bottom of the rib-cage starts), downward toward the pubic bone. After several of these, bring your hands to the back of your lover's waist, and draw them around the waist, following the line of the groin down toward the pubic bone. Use several long sweeping strokes to relax the muscles here.*

The following meditation can then be done lying or sitting. You can watch your partner as a witness, leading him or her through the visualization and encouraging them to soften their belly, or you can do the meditation together.

◆ *If sitting, get comfortable and bring your attention to the physical sensations in your body. Feel your head on your spine, and your spine aligned with all the vertebra stacked up in your back. Relax your body, without drooping. Bring*

your awareness to your breath. As you breathe in and out for some minutes, relax and let your breath breathe itself.

◆ *Slow your breathing right down and let each breath sink into your belly. Allow your belly to rise with every inhalation, and fall with every exhalation. Sit comfortably. Keep breathing into your belly until you lose track of time. It may help to close your eyes.*

◆ *Draw your breath from your lungs down into your abdomen. Hold your breath, allowing it to sit in the base of your abdomen. Imagine a ball of light and heat, like a sun sitting in your belly and warming it. Let your belly absorb the warmth, softening and relaxing in the sun's heat. Encourage the warm rays of the sun to spread through your body and limbs, making them relaxed and languid. Allow the warm light of the sun to diffuse outwards, softening your whole being.*

◆ *Once you are fully relaxed, let the bright light of the sun's rays illuminate a moon, shimmering as it comes into focus. Notice that the crescent moon is nestling inside the sun, and its clear light sends a refreshing cool breeze out of your belly.*

◆ *Breathe in this cool breeze, laden with the nourishing rays of the moon and the sun. Soften your belly as the rays of the sun and moon entwine together to fill your being.*

30

·•·

OPENING TO JOY

 The purpose of your relationship is to give each
other joy, letting your Beloved find joy in your body
as well as in their own.

Tantric texts describe the movement toward the ultimate goal of bliss in love-making as an ever more subtle
unfolding of your capacity for joy. The way you make love
depends on the degree to which you can deliver yourself to
joy. By activating your subtle body during love-making, you
can open to joy.

In Tantra, "innate joy" manifests itself in four stages during
love-making:

1. Smile At the first stage of love-making when your emo-
   tions are stimulated through connection, joy manifests as
   a smile; a sign of the contentment that emotional intimacy
   brings. The play of emotions between you expresses itself

in the variety of your play and exploration of each other's bodies.

2. *Gaze The next stage is called "perfect joy", when joy is deepened through your gaze (see page 90). Look at your partner and see their body as a yantra, or power form (see page 226), and your own bodies conjoined as a power form.*

3. *Embrace The consummation of your sexual attraction and desire through your bodies' embracing is described as "absolute joy".*

4. *Divine union The ultimate Tantric goal is "innate joy", where your sexual union transcends your two bodies pleasuring one another, and enters the realm of the divine. Tantric teachers regard joy as innate, and have developed the techniques used in this book to help you access it.*

Ritual

Before you start tonight's love-making, sit together in a smiling meditation. Close your eyes and imagine your belly smiling. It's a warm feeling of wellbeing and contentment. Let the smile spread throughout your internal organs and climb into your face. Feel your face soften with the smile.

- ◆ *Think how you long to make your lover smile, and how much you love it when you see that your presence lights up their life. Spend a few minutes thinking about all the ways you make them laugh, and the different types of their smile; mysterious, lavish, gentle, tantalizing, sarcastic, shy … think about the things that encourage you both to enter the joy of these emotions. Feel your emotions rising from your belly.*

- ◆ *Open your eyes and gaze at each other with smiling eyes (see page 90). Really look at your partner's mouth, and drink in the smile playing on their lips. See how their eyes light up as they behold you. Allow the sight of their enjoyment of you to penetrate your consciousness; absorb the joy of being loved and desired. Embrace each other as lovers, focusing on generating joy through gifting each other your pleasure.*

- ◆ *During love-making, focus on the descent of energy from your head. Allow the delightful sensations of your body to claim your full attention. Stop thinking and focus on your body, reveling in the perfection of this moment.*

- ◆ *As you move into a quieter phase in your love-making, focus on absorbing the delight generated through your*

love-play. Open your heart to each other. Concentrate on drawing this pool of delight and joy up through your chakras into your forehead. Don't enter a thinking, observing mode. Instead, you're fully immersed in delight, and you are using the energy generated through pleasure to nourish your energy-body.

◆ Hover at the edge of orgasm without succumbing to it, as this will keep you in a high state of arousal. Allow this excitement to expand until it becomes a feeling of bliss – in uniting with your lover, you are uniting with the Beloved. Through uniting with your Beloved, you access an experience of becoming one with the universe.

31

·•·

POST-COITAL MEDITATION

We were wrapped in each other's arms, completely in sympathy. It felt deeply harmonious; a place where all our petty power struggles were washed away. It was like lying in the ocean, deep and profound, yet without any fear. Like letting go of the need to assert ourselves as individual and separate, instead merging without any suffocating co-dependency. The feelings we are so afraid of in day-to-day life just seem easy and natural. It's a place I want to return to as much as possible.

 It is important to remain physically close after orgasm, to deepen the bonding process. Leave the lingam (penis) and yoni (vagina) joined together so that your love juices are mixed and energy is exchanged, which will have a revitalizing effect on you both and nourish you psychically.

This is an unstructured exercise in which you meditate in the space after orgasm, with one partner acting as guide for the other. Meditation connects you with the source of unconditional love and enables you to open yourself to receive love, as well as giving it. Regular meditation gives you access to the nature of existence, which mystics describe as divine love. Regular meditation with your partner will nurture your relationship and create a firm bond between you.

Instead of consigning your sexual climax to the wasteland of the "little death", or post-coital let-down that often follows sex, use this internalized mood to enter an active state of meditation. Meditation is the door through which you enter altered states of consciousness. During sex you may have approached an altered state, and meditating afterward will consolidate that experience.

Ritual

Allow yourself to fall into a state of deep relaxation, without going to sleep. The other partner can speak to you just sufficiently to stop you dropping off to sleep, by prompting you to describe your state.

Lie together, focusing on harmonizing your energy bodies (see spoon ritual, page 236), or lie together with your heart wide open, full of love for your partner.

Observe any sensations, emotions, images or fantasies that arise as you enter this state of meditation. Alternatively, you may be in a state of non-thinking and emptiness (a release from normal waking thought processes), an altered awareness, or a state of bliss. As associations, feeling states, fantasies, and images come up, describe them to your partner, who listens without comment or interpretation, acting as a witness. Allow images to arise spontaneously during the meditation, and share them afterwards with your partner. The process of finding words to express your experience and share it with your partner connects you consciously, as well as the energy connection you have already created during this breath meditation.

When you are in this state of reverie and loving attentiveness, you can discuss your experiences after the meditation, or the following morning.

Variation

If you need a guided meditation try the following. Here, you use visualization to cocoon your lover in the embrace of love.

◆ *Start with relaxation and deepening the breath.*

◆ *Imagine your own body and that of your lover lying as if in a cocoon, wrapped in a ball of golden light. Then, visualize a clear, emerald-green light in the heart area of your chest, which gradually permeates both your bodies and expands to color the golden ball a bright emerald green. Emerald is the color of the heart, and of the Tantric Buddhist goddess, Tara.*

◆ *While floating in the universal heart of your beloved, focus on the oneness in which we are all connected.*

32

FORGIVENESS MEDITATION

 This exercise is about healing your past wounds and present confusions. Your relationship is a vehicle for mutual healing, on physical, emotional, and soul levels. You need to embrace any emotional pain or mental anguish that comes up as part of the work of your relationship.

In their excellent book *Embracing the Beloved*, authors Stephen and Ondrea Levine suggest that attempts to get away from your own pain and grief end up creating distance between yourself and your partner. To heal it, they suggest that you open up to your own pain, so as to dissolve in the compassion of your loving heart. Accepting your own pain enables you to feel this compassion. Compassion *is* love.

Ritual

Start by thinking about all the grudges and resentments you have about your partner. Write down all the ways you feel they have hurt you or let you down. In your mind's eye, you will forgive them for every one.

◆ *Begin with a namaste, bowing to your partner.*

◆ *Sit in front of your partner. Feel your love. Gaze at them with soft eyes full of loving kindness. Allow your love to dissolve any resentments or hurt you are holding on to.*

◆ *Say in your heart, or out loud: "I forgive you." Concentrate on forgiving your lover for anything they may have done to hurt you, whether intentionally or not. You may want to visualise yourself offering them a flower as a token of your forgiveness.*

◆ *With every breath, draw their mercy into your heart, and send them forgiveness. Experience the forgiveness as a bridge that links your two hearts. Sit gazing at each other for several minutes, resting in the atmosphere of love you have generated through compassion.*

◆ *You may want to include the angelic heart meditation on page 27.*

33

•◆•

CONTEMPLATING COMPASSION

 In order to really see the divine in others, you need to concentrate on opening your heart in compassion. This allows you a true sense of another's suffering; in relationship terms, seeing yourselves as fellow travelers struggling through life means you recognize your fundamental sameness.

Ritual

◆ *Sit comfortably, and bring your attention to your breath filling your lungs and emptying. Let it settle into a slow, gentle breath. Focus on the breath breathing itself. Feel a sense of wonder at your body for the miracle of breathing.*

◆ *Feel thankful for your body, and appreciate it. Thank it for the help and pleasure it gives you. Feel kindly toward its aches and weaknesses. Send healing breath into any areas that feel uncomfortable.*

◆ *Sit with this healing breath radiating your body for several moments. Feel how your body expands with the love.*

- *Feel love in your heart, and allow it to spread through your whole being. With each in-breath, feel your heart opening like a rosebud. With each out-breath, allow the beauty of that open rose to permeate your body.*

- *After several minutes, bring your partner to mind. Or if they are sitting in front of you, open your eyes slowly and gaze at them with loving kindness.*

- *With each in-breath, feel your heart opening like a bud. With each out-breath, send out your love toward them. Feel the loving connection created between you and your breaths, and as you breathe out send out the intention that their heart flowers. See their struggle for happiness, and acknowledge that they are just like you. Look on the ways they express their difficulties and struggle with compassion. They are doing the best they can, just as you are trying to do your best to find happiness. Feel this compassion filling your heart.*

- *With every out-breath, send out waves of compassion. Send out vitality and healing toward your partner. With your out-breath, say the words, "may you be free of suffering," voicing them in your heart or out loud.*

- *Close the meditation with a warm, loving embrace.*

34

SEXUAL HEALING: GIVE YOUR
GENITALS A VOICE

 Consider your genitals as your whole being, rather than a part that can be misunderstood or taken for granted. Just as your sexuality is fundamental to your being, so your genitals influence the way you experience your body.

If you have experienced sexual wounding or ambivalence in the past, these experiences will cause defensiveness, or body-armoring, in the genitals, which needs to be released before you can open fully to erotic pleasure. It is very healing to share these experiences with your partner in an atmosphere of loving acceptance. You will be able to release the negative charge of emotions held in your body.

This is an exercise in healing. It can be very challenging, but if you can manage to be honest and caring with one another, your relationship will grow enormously in trust.

Ritual

You can do this exercise on your own, or together with your partner.

◆ *Draw a large picture of your genitals. Through the process of drawing, feel your way into your genitals. What is your shape and color? What is your mood? Imagine yourself as your lingam or yoni. How does it make you feel when you totally identify yourself with your sexual organs?*

◆ *Once you have drawn your genitals, reflect on the illustration and recall the experiences you have gone through, from the perspective of your genitals. If you wish to share your process with her or him, give your genitals a voice. Talk about your past sexual experiences from the point of view of your genitals. Resist the desire to giggle, as this exercise needs to be conducted with great sensitivity.*

◆ *Listen with compassionate attention to your lover's description of their past sexual experiences and how they have felt. Your role is that of an active listener; listening with full attention. Be receptive and non-judgmental, and let go of any jealous or competitive emotions that may arise.*

Your partner may be sharing experiences that were joyful and rapturous, or they may be talking about episodes that were painful or humiliating. They may express their grief about times when sex was not heart-full enough. Allow this sorrow to be expressed in tears or anger, or any other way it comes to the surface. Old griefs may have led to a loss of joy and creativity or a progressive closing down to love and sex. Perhaps they have shaped familiar patterns of relating to your own sexuality or to others. In order to be healed, it helps if your emotions are released in the safety of a loving witness.

TO THE WOMAN

Consider the following:

- *How did it feel to be your yoni and hunger for loving kindness, pleasure, or erotic satisfaction?*
- *How did it feel to receive the energy of a phallus?*
- *How did you feel if you made love when you weren't properly aroused, or when your partner ejaculated, leaving you sexually frustrated?*

TO THE MAN

Consider the following:

◆ *How did it feel to be a man, attempting to satisfy your sexual partners or give them orgasms?*

◆ *How did it feel to take your pleasure? How did it feel to be received by your partner? How did it feel to monitor your own performance, instead of getting lost in pleasure?*

To close this exercise, describe how you would like your sexual experience to be changed. If you find certain aspects of your relationship healing, mention these as well as saying if there is anything else that you need from your lover. You may want to include a compassion meditation (see page 113).

Your breath is the breath of life. In Tantra, breath is key to channeling energy through your body.

In this exercise, you take turns to use your breath to stimulate your lover's energy-body, which permeates and surrounds their physical body, increasing sensitivity.

Ritual

◆ *Start by sitting in quiet meditation. Allow your respiration to settle into a long, slow rhythm, gently rising and falling. As you breathe in, draw the energizing breath into your heart, warming it with your love before exhaling.*

◆ *With your inner eye, see your lover sitting before you. Visualize your breath surrounding him or her with loving energy, warming your lover's heart and encouraging him or her to grow radiantly luminous.*

◆ *Open your eyes and gaze at your lover. With each exhalation, bathe his or her form with the loving energy of your*

breath. With your heartful breath, blow softly on your lover's skin, caressing your lover with loving emanations from your mouth. Keeping your breath deep and tender, hover with your lips just an inch or so above the flesh.

◆ Blow from the base of the spine, between the buttocks, up to the base of the head. Then blow from your lover's buttocks down their outstretched legs. Waft him or her into a state of deep relaxation as your breath permeates their being, caressing the energy-body. Breathe out along the energy channels running from the heart down to the navel, and from the navel down to the genitals. Breathe in the fire energy around the yoni (vulva and vagina) or lingam (penis), allowing it to fill your being, then blow this energy back over the body, allowing your exhalation to caress the belly, top of the breasts, throat, lips, and finally the forehead.

◆ Once the energy channels in your lover's body that link sex, the heart, and the psyche have been enlivened, explore blowing on different parts of the body. Play with your breath over your lover's fingertips, earlobes, nape of the neck, and inside of the knees. Your partner can then caress you with their breath.

36

SEVEN-STEP ENERGY MASSAGE

 The key to Tantric massage is to enliven the body. Its true purpose is not relaxation for its own sake, but to energize the body while your lover is in a state of surrendered relaxation, which creates a deep trust between you.

The aim of this massage is to include the energy-body as well as the physical body in sensual massage. This massage moves through seven steps, treating your energy and physical bodies as different modes.

Ritual

Light a candle, and put on some soft background music, if you like. Wash your hands before starting the massage. Water is a purifier, and helps you get rid of negative energy.

Sit in silence for a few moments, centering yourself (see page xx). Your partner can lie on their back or front for this exercise.

◆ *Massage the aura: the aura extends outside the body. This prepares your energy-body for the experience of massage. Hold your hands with palms outstretched about an inch over your lover's body. Start at the base of the spine and run your hands above their spine, hovering over the skin. Use circular movements at the base of the spine, expanding the movements to long, upward sweeps as you start to move the energy upward. Use circular movements again in the area of the heart, between their shoulder blades. Hold your hands over the occiput – these are the bones at the base of the head, where it sits on the neck vertebrae. Focus on releasing the tension at this point. Your partner can discharge negative energy by visualizing dark, polluted air coming out with each exhalation. Go back to the tailbone at the base of the spine, and work on stroking the energy-body above the sacrum. Then work on the arms and legs, sweeping away from the body.*

◆ *Affirming touch: Next, use an affirming touch to make contact with the body and define their physical form through touch. Lightly smooth the skin, making contact with your lover's physical body. Pay particular attention to the areas around the sacrum, navel, heart, throat, and third eye, especially if they are lying on their back.*

◆ *Applying pressure: The next step is to go deeper, pressing into soft tissues under the skin. Apply firm pressure as you both breathe in, and hold it, allowing your partner to release any tension held in the muscles and become still under your hands. Gently release the pressure, so that your partner remains relaxed as you remove your hands. Breathe slowly and deeply together, relaxing into this sense of stillness.*

◆ *Plucking: Energize the body with a fast plucking action. Imagine that you are pulling out any negative energy in the body. This is also stimulating and enlivening. Be playful as you let the energy rise.*

◆ *Light touching: Once your body feels tingly with the stimulation, arouse sensitivity with slow light touch. You are barely touching the skin with your fingertips. The slower the better – as a slow touch is even more sensitive than a firm one.*

◆ *Using a feather: Next, make your massage touch even finer by using a feather. Run a feather across their skin so lightly that the very tip of the feather barely bends.*

- *Experimenting with sensations: Now eroticize the stimulation even more, while keeping it fine. Use your hair, or a silk scarf to trail across the flesh. Blow on your lover with your breath. Experiment with sensations of coolness and warmth, with a cold sponge or a heated herbal pillow perfumed with lavender.*
- *Finish with freestyle massage, or go back to the massage your partner most enjoyed and play with that.*

37

SOLAR MASSAGE, LUNAR MASSAGE

 Water is the source of life. In the outer world the white force, or moon, is the female lunar principle, or water element. On an inner level, the inner moon becomes male, Shiva, while Shakti, the female, is the source of fire and passion. Our bodies are comprised of masculine and feminine elements which used to be integrated.

Here is a solar massage for the god, Shiva, and a lunar massage for Shakti, the goddess. We are influenced by both solar and lunar heavenly bodies, so you may choose to do either of these massages.

You concentrate on these qualities in order to develop them in yourselves. In these meditations you identify with the energy emanating from the sun and moon, by stimulating the site of these energies in your partner's body.

Shiva's solar energy massage

◆ Shakti (the female partner) sits in contemplation on the flame of a floating candle. In the flickering flame, visualize your partner as Shiva, all-powerful and loving Lord of the universe. Your partner visualizes himself as a living god. He concentrates on an image of the sun filling his navel, whose flames rise up to lick his whole being.

◆ Gaze at your partner's body. Worship him as the sun god, resplendent in his glory. Trace the energy channels in his body with your fingertips, following a line that starts at his left toe, moving to his knee, thigh, lingam (penis), rolling around to stroke his left buttock before coming back to his belly, to his navel, and up to the middle of his chest. Let your hand rest on his breast-bone for a few moments, contacting his heart. Visualize energy streaming out from your fingertips, arousing him.

◆ Follow the energy channel across to his right breast before going down his arm to the fingers and back up again, moving up his neck to the throat, his lower lip, right cheek, eye, and forehead to the top of the head. Then trace the parallel channels on his left side. These are his lunar energy channels.

- *Then begin to stroke his lingam (penis), navel, heart, and thighs with increasingly erotic intent. While you touch these areas, link them with the palms of his hands, his feet, and his forehead.*
- *Use scented massage oil to oil his genitals, navel, throat, forehead, and top of his head, visualizing him as your potent and loving divine partner.*
- *If he's aroused and you'd like to make love, straddle him while he lies back and continues to enjoy your ministrations. While in this position, he focuses on building up solar energy in navel (imagining the sun, or flames licking at his belly), while you channel energy through your hands onto the solar channels of the body. Keep massaging his navel, scrotum, and perineum, chest and forehead, while riding him.*

Shakti's lunar energy massage

- *Trace the lunar energy channel in your lover's body; from right toe to the knee, thigh, yoni (vulva and vagina), buttock, navel, middle of chest, right breast, arm, throat, right cheek, lower lip, eye, and top of her head. Then trace down the left-sided channels. Visualize energy streaming from your fingertips, stimulating her passion.*

◆ *Worship your lover as the moon goddess, in order to appreciate her divine nature. See her as the luminous heavenly body she is, looking beyond her everyday familiarity to glimpse her mystery. Shakti, imagine a deep well of love between your breasts, the source of bountiful love for yourself and others. This is the numinous source of the mystery of the heart.*

◆ *Meanwhile, Shakti visualizes herself as a living goddess, full of love, Shiva's crucible to transform their passion. She stimulates herself by deep breathing and by gently rocking her pelvis back and forth, encouraging the Kundalini energy (the universal energy at the base of her spine) to rise up and fill her being with a charged energy.*

◆ *Apply massage oil scented with her favorite essential oil to her pubic hair, navel, throat, forehead, and top of her head, saying, "water becomes fire. Sexual energy is the flame. In this fire, I offer up my semen. Fire becomes water. Woman's love-juices are the food for life."*

◆ *As if you were anointing a goddess, rub perfume or scented water behind her ears, and the palms of her hands, calling her your beloved over and over again.*

38

•✦•

FOOT MASSAGE

Care of the feet is a devotional act, both intimate and nurturing. Attending to your partner's feet makes them feel loved and cared for. It may be appropriate if your partner is feeling stressed, fatigued or burdened to demonstrate your support by tending to their feet, which literally support them standing up and being active in the world.

Ritual

◆ *Set up an altar and light a candle for contemplation.*

◆ *Start the exercise by honoring your partner as the god Shiva, or goddess Shakti, bowing to them.*

◆ *Invite your lover to soak their feet in a bowl of salted water, relaxing by watching a single candle flame. Seat them comfortably and bring them the bowl of warm, salted water, and place their feet in it.*

◆ *Let them sit quietly in meditation at this time. Leave to prepare some food for later, making it with devotion.*

- *After fifteen or twenty minutes, dry your lover's feet with a towel. Invite them to make themselves comfortable on some cushions.*

- *Honor your lover as the great god Shiva or the goddess Shakti. Drape a soft white shawl over his shoulders, or loosely tie a red silk scarf around her waist. Acknowledge him or her as your perfect lover. Massage the feet and toes with perfumed oil. While massaging them, hum a mantra to yourself (see page 78), sing songs of praise or love songs to your beloved.*

- *Massage their feet with massage oil or almond oil, perfumed with an essential oil of your choice. Massage gently at first, then more firmly, exploring all the different parts: the instep, toes, between the toes, soles, and Achilles tendon. Experiment with different strokes and pressures, using your fingertips and palms. Ask your partner to let you know if you are causing any pain – that's not the object of this exercise.*

- *Channel your own healing and revitalizing energy from your heart through your hands as you are doing the massage. Your lover can focus on receiving your loving energy through your hands.*

39

· ◆ ·

BREAST MASSAGE

 Breasts are an area of the body that expresses women's primary positive pole. This means that her heart area between the breasts is active, whereas men's heart center may need activating through love. The heart center is situated between the breasts, and stimulating the breasts arouses love. For this reason, the breast massage is also good for men.

This exercise is not a prelude to love-making, but a joyful exploration of a primary erogenous zone, both physically and energetically. Focus on the breast as a site of pleasure.

Ritual

◆ *Begin with a namaste (see page 2).*

◆ *Uncover your lover's breasts slowly, with tenderness and grace. Gaze at your lover's breasts. Give her some appreciative feedback or create devotional songs about her gorgeous breasts.*

◆ *Start by concentrating on the heart region between your lover's breasts. Touch the breasts tentatively, barely grazing them with your breath, fingertips or eyelashes as you expand to the breasts, exploring the nipples, breasts, the sides of the breast, and up under the armpit. Tease them with brief contact, moving toward the breasts or nipples and away over the chest and belly. Try feathers, fabrics, fingertips, tongue, hair, or the bristles on your chin to stroke and caress your lover's breasts. Try out different pressures, touches. Ask her whether she prefers less pressure, or she likes it harder, softer, faster, slower.*

◆ *Explore the nipples with your tongue, then blow gently on the wet skin. Enjoy the nipples with exotic fruit, such as mango, avocado, and honey.*

◆ *Tantric practitioners believe the breasts emit a sacred fluid when aroused, which should be ingested. So suck and lick your lover's breasts, ingesting any moisture as nourishment.*

If you are receiving the massage, just concentrate on the pleasure and allow yourself to drop into the subtle physical sensations. Tell your partner whether you prefer to be stroked, squeezed, licked, or nibbled.

40

PENIS REFLEXOLOGY

 Reflexologists have mapped zones on the surface of the body that correlate with internal channels of subtle energy. They stimulate these through massage techniques to revitalize the energy within your body.

Just as the energy channels of the body can be mapped on the feet, the face, the hands, and the ears, they can also be mapped on the penis. The penis is a long column that mirrors your spine, the location of the central energy channel, or inner flute (see page 176). Energy is concentrated at different intervals along this channel. In this exercise, you explore the points along your partner's lingam (penis) that can stimulate these different energies. You will be creating your own energy map through experimentation, as the reflexology zones of the penis have yet to be fully mapped.

Exploring the energy correlation between your penis and your inner flute helps you become more sensitive to the subtle sensations produced by stimulating different areas of your penis. You can do this by using the chakra meditation while receiving the massage (see page 52).

Ritual

Open the exercise with a chakra meditation (see page 236). Do this together, to focus your attention on the chakras, and then open your intuitive faculties. This meditation gets you in touch with your energy-body, rather than focusing on the physical sensations of having your penis stimulated.

After the chakra meditation, visualize red drops at base of your penis as blood coursing through the channels of your body (see solar massage, page 125) becoming mixed with the wind of your breath and transformed into white drops at the tip of your penis. Do this during the chakra massage, working through each of the penis chakras (see box on page 134).

Don't worry too much about exactly where the points are supposed to be. Just massage at close intervals from the very bottom to the tip. Your partner will tell you what feels good or interesting. Play with these chakra points by spreading your fingers in a ring around his penis, gently squeezing and massaging your way up his lingam from the base.

THE LINGAM CHAKRA POINTS

Just like the seven chakras (wheels of energy) located up the spine, there are seven corresponding sites located along the lingam, starting at its root. Where the penis emerges from deep inside the muscles under the perineum (the area between the scrotum and anus) is the site that corresponds to the base chakra. The second chakra is around the base of the penis, just behind where it joins the scrotum. The area where the foreskin joins the glans (forming a v-shape on the underside of the head of the lingam) corresponds to the brow chakra. The area at the tip of the glans, where the semen exits, corresponds to the crown chakra. You can explore the shaft of the penis to find out where the other two points are, which depends on the shape and size of your penis.

135 ❀

41

***

AWAKENING THE SENSE OF SMELL

Smell is the sense associated with the root, or base chakra, your instinctual aspect. This is the home of the Kundalini, your vital force. Smell can be used to stimulate your vitality.

In India, sweet-smelling scents, herbs, and oils are associated with the root chakra, and are used to arouse erotic energy; women perfume their own bodies and also anoint their lover's bodies with sandalwood paste. You can use scent throughout your love rituals – for instance, anointing your male partner with massage oil, and garlanding his head with a crown of fresh flowers and leaves (ivy is a useful plant to use as a base from which to construct a natural crown). You could decide to sweeten the room where you make love with fresh flowers, sweet-smelling perfumes, essential oils, or incense.

This ritual stimulates your partner with individual scents to heighten sensitivity. Prepare for the exercise beforehand so that your partner can just relax and concentrate on what is happening in the present moment, without thoughts or expectations. Think about a range of olfactory stimulations – unusual and interesting smells. Arrange a group of items that have different smells: foodstuffs such as a cut lemon, flowers, perfumes, or oils.

Ritual

Settle your beloved into a comfortable nest in a room, illuminated with only one or two candles so that he or she cannot see the source of the smell sensation. Let them be tantalized by the smell without trying to work out where it is coming from. They may prefer to have their eyes covered with a blindfold. Pass essential oils under your partner's nose without touching the skin. Allow him or her to inhale, and then wait a minute or two before offering the next smell sensation.

Peppermint or eucalyptus essential oils are good to start with. After that, use sweeter and more mysterious essences, such as lotus, ylang-ylang, and gardenia. You can also play music that incorporates the sounds of running water or waves splashing, and spray a fine mist of scented water over your lover's head.

Variation

Close your eyes and smell your lover. Inhale their body scent. Smell the nape of the neck, between the breasts, the navel, and thighs. Like an animal, forage those places where their body gives off a strong scent; sniff under their arms and between their legs. Play at being an animal, seeking out your mate's scents.

Inhale your lover's smells deeply. Take them into your body, allowing them to physically nourish your relationship. Then anoint your lover's body with different essential oils to discover for yourself how each one affects his or her natural scents, and how it affects both of you. Experiment with pure essential oils to see which ones correspond to the different parts of their body. Anoint the back of their ears, forehead, the nape of the neck, hollows of the shoulders, breasts, and navel … try essences of rose, jasmine, amber, myrrh, or lavender.

THE CHAKRAS AND THE SENSES

Tantrics develop sensory awareness through paying attention to the sensations discovered by their five senses, as well as to the five primary elements thought to make up the world; earth, water, fire, air, and ether. These correspond to the first five chakras. The chakras can be stimulated by awakening the sense associated with each element:

Chakra	Location	Sense
1. Root (muladhara)	Base of spine	Smell
2. Sexual (svadisthana)	Genitals	Taste
3. Solar plexus (manipura)	Solar plexus	Sight
4. Heart (anahata)	Heart	Touch
5. Throat chakra (vissudha)	Throat	Hearing
6. Brow chakra (ajna)	Third eye	The mind
7. Crown center (sahasrara)	Top of head	Incorporating all senses; lost in bliss

·•·

42

AWAKENING THE SENSE OF HEARING

I used to feel cynical or upset when I heard a particular soundtrack with children laughing. Perhaps it reminded me of my own unhappiness as a child, and as a result I didn't think it sounded genuine. Now that I have children, I appreciate these sounds of happiness and I regard laughter as their birthright.

Hearing is connected with the throat chakra, the energy center responsible for expression as well as hearing. It is also associated with the sacred sense of awareness (see box), which is awakened by sound. Stimulate your sense of hearing by listening to laughter, song, and harmonious music.

Ritual

◆ *You can awaken your auditory sense by focusing your awareness on the sound of your own breath. To tune yourself to your lover, listen to his or her breath.*

◆ *Experience the pleasure of humming. Chant your lover's name over and over again as a mantra, or use a mantra (see page 78) to focus your awareness through the sense of sound.*

◆ *If you have any musical instruments such as bells, cymbals, flutes or maracas you can use these. Begin by introducing just one sound, making it as continuous and as resonant as possible. For instance, ring a bell and move it around your partner at different distances while it reverberates. Otherwise, you can use short excerpts of beautiful, evocative music. Choose your favorite atmospheric music – gentle and relaxing, or lyrical.*

◆ *After a moment's silence, change the music to something that makes you both feel full of love. Sitting behind your partner, gently rest your hand on their heart. Allow them to lean back on you, feeling your warmth.*

THE SEVEN SACRED SENSES

In Tantra, there are seven sacred senses:

Sense	Is awakened through:
1. Awareness	Sound
2. Discrimination	Smell
3. Assimilation	Food
4. Surrender	Heartful relaxation
5. Balance	Visualization
6. Vision	Soul connection
7. Unification	Universal connection

The awakening exercises (see pages 136–51) also stimulate the five senses we're more familiar with: hearing (through music), smell (scents and essential oils), taste (food and drink), touch (stroking with feathers), and sight (when you remove the blindfold to look at each other, and the beautiful objects your partner has used and then arranged). The senses are delighted and stimulated through offerings, flowers, candlelight, incense, chimes, and fragrances such as rose water.

43

⋅•⋅

AWAKENING THE SENSE OF TASTE

 Refresh and rejuvenate your lover during prolonged bouts of love-making. Light food, made from vegetables and grains, is considered best before embarking on an evening of love-making. Spicy foods arouse passions as they are linked to the element of fire: meals containing lots of red meat, garlic, onion, and chilli. Consider which qualities you would like to encourage in your love-making when preparing food.

Sacramental food becomes "charged" during its ritual preparation. You can meditate while cooking, or sing. Whether you are preparing a meal for your lover, refreshments for love-making, or tidbits to stimulate his or her senses, take time to prepare it. Immerse yourself in what you are doing, taking care to think about what your lover would find appetizing. Think about what would be adventurous, exciting, stimulating, or unexpected. Spend an hour or more on this exercise, leaving a minute or two between each stimulus.

Ritual

Introduce your lover to a delectable range of taste sensations. Encourage them to relax, breathe deeply and enjoy the experiences you are offering. There is no need to talk, unless they wish to share their impressions. Ask them to close their eyes or be blindfolded.

Playfully offer small, bite-sized portions of exotic fruit, like avocado, mango, star fruit, passion, or kiwi fruit to your partner's mouth. Offer a glass of sparkling elderflower wine or cordial (you'll need a straw for your partner to take a sip if they are blindfolded.) After a minute or two, offer the next taste sensation.

For example, you can dip a grape into some liqueur and let your partner smell it. After a moment, caress the lips with the grape before teasingly offering it to their mouth – and finally press it to the lips until they part and allow it to go in, ever so slowly. Dip your finger into the liqueur and caress your partner's lips with it. Offer food from your own mouth, mixed with your own saliva.

44

AWAKENING THE SENSE OF SIGHT

Sight is connected to the energy center in the region of your solar plexus, and the element of fire. Vision is directly responsible for arousing the heat of your passion, so delight your lover's eyes with a series of visions.

Ritual

◆ *Prepare the room for a total visual experience. Arrange it as your idea of paradise, or a haven. Light candles and incense, and place a tray with snacks and delicacies in the center of the room, along with any other objects you wish to show them. You can create an aesthetic arrangement with them.*

◆ *Blindfold your partner and gently lead them into the room, reassuring them that there is no need to talk. Covering your lover's eyes with a scarf will reduce distractions and intensify the experience.*

◆ *Silently remove your partner's blindfold, and look at each other and the objects you have displayed. Instead of an*

active gaze, where you are looking at objects in an ana-
lytical way, focus on receiving the image of the objects into
your eyes. Just let them be as they are, without trying to
understand them. It helps if you soften your gaze and con-
centrate your whole being on becoming receptive. Talk to
each other about what you see.

◆ *Close the ritual with a long, tender hug. Sit in connection,*
allowing the sensory experiences you have shared to bind
you closely as a sensual couple.

My lover led me blindfold into our living room and sat me in a
nest of cushions near the fireplace. He delighted me by
touching me delicately, in unexpected ways. He tantalized me
with intense smells and extraordinary tastes. After a surprising
journey through my senses, we sat quietly holding hands,
enjoying the warmth of the fire. When he slipped the scarf
from my eyes, I explored all the things he had used with a sense
of wonder. The whole experience was one of simple delight.

45

AWAKENING THE SENSE OF TOUCH

Ecstasy is a state of being, it's a feeling of being at one with myself, and inhabiting my body. It's a sense of aliveness, when I feel energy streaming inside me like little pulsations here and there. There's a warm glow around my heart, and a free and open feeling in my chest and in my mind. The area around my third eye – between my brows – feels sensitive.

Tantra is concerned with allowing more sensitivity, to fully experience what's already there. The simple sensation of soft touch on your skin can be extremely powerful. Reclaiming the sensitivity of the body is important for healing. It helps you to reconnect with and strengthen the energetic aspects of sex. This exercise heightens awareness, opening your body and mind to love and excitement. It encourages you to develop your sensitivity, moving away from a libidinal drive for sexual sensation.

Ritual

Place an array of interestingly textured objects in a large bag or basket for your partner to reach into and handle. To select the objects, go around your home trying out different textures on the inside of your arm to see how they feel. For instance, you might select a soft brush, some feathers, a meat tenderizer, the bristles of a paintbrush, a sponge. Children's bubbles or shaving foam might be interesting. Be imaginative.

When you are offering these objects to your partner, you could touch different surfaces of their body, varying the speed and pressure of your contact. Try the lightest and most tentative touch first. Brush the skin first with a piece of fur, then with feather, silk or other textured fabrics. Move it slowly and delicately across their cheeks, neck, and arms – or wrists and ankles. Seduce your partner with your loving intent.

Your partner concentrates on opening their heart to receiving the sensory experiences you are offering them. They can focus on incorporating the energy of each sensory stimulation into the heart chakra.

46

UPPER LIP MEDITATION

I lay back on the waterbed like a water lily floating in a wide
expanse, my heart open like a precious flower. His lips
hovered over my half-closed buds, seeking sustenance. I felt
that my heart had enough for both of us.

In mapping the energy-body (see page 48), Tantric
texts describe a channel between the clitoris and
upper lip. The clitoris is one of a woman's solar sexual zones,
corresponding to the head of a man's penis (see page 300).

This meditation helps women increase the energetic connections to their clitoris. It helps to be able to focus on the
energy-body during love-making, as well as the pleasurable
sensations that arise from pleasuring the clitoris.

Ritual

You may want to start this exercise with a meditation to harmonize the chakras, such as reciting a mantra (see page 74).

Start by relaxing your whole body through deep breathing. (You may want to play tranquil music to help you relax completely.) As your breath slows and lengthens, find a place of stillness in both body and mind. Begin to focus on the subtle processes of your energy body. Visualize a lotus flower at the crown of your head. Another lotus sits on your upper lip. The roots of the lotus are wrapped around your vulva, which looks like a shell. The long, delicate stem rises up through your body to the crown of your head. From there it arches down between your eyes and behind your nose, coming to a rest at your upper lip.

As you breathe in, imagine this stem drawing water from its roots into the delicate tendrils over your upper lip. Breathe in slowly and deeply as you visualize drawing this nurturing water upward with each breath, nourishing your lips with minerals and nutrients from the deep bed of the lake.

⋅•⋅

47

WORSHIP YOUR LOVER WITH
DEVOTION: THE PRACTICE OF PUJA

 A strong, erotic attraction between you and your partner may be an expression of your yearning for mystical union with a soul mate. Your sexual attraction to one another can give power to your spiritual life as a couple. In Tantra, your sexual chemistry fuels an alchemical transformation of the erotic energy between you.

Your sexual attraction also helps you develop caring, loving, devotional qualities, grounding these in everyday selflessness, such as when you put your partner first. Doing this in a devotional ritual, or puja, creates bonds of love and compassion.

Through the practice of devotion, you deepen your love. Worshipping your lover as your soul mate, or beloved, means that you worship the divine in them. The divine stands for the inherently lovely, lovable, and loving in human nature.

In worshipping your partner, you acknowledge his or her true nature as love. We are all divine in essence, if only we can uncover our love. You can help each other to do so through the devotional practice of puja.

Ritual

This night's practice is to serve your partner with devotion. Prepare the room as your temple space for the night. Cleanse it with fresh water, scattering rose petals, or cleanse the air with burning sage. Invoke the spirits of the divine lovers (Shakti and Shiva) through prayer or meditation. Light candles or incense before welcoming your beloved, seating him or her comfortably and offering water laced with herbs or fruit. Offer your partner flowers and perfumes, and dainties such as honeyed yogurt or sweetmeats. Traditional Tantric practitioners ritually wash different parts of their body, including the mouth and nose. You may lovingly bathe your lover's body, or wash his or her feet with scented water. Massage the feet or breasts or delight them with a seven-step energy massage (see pages 120–31). You may wish to close the ritual by robing them (see page 290).

I'm independent and self-contained. It's a challenge for me to let myself be part of a team – to allow her to share my worries, and learn to listen to her feelings. Serving her has softened me and enabled me to receive more from her.

48

DANCING BACK TO BACK

"Please be ready for me at eight."

"Would you like me to cook dinner?"

I wanted to make my intentions clear. "No, I don't want to eat – well, not unless it's snacks we can eat in bed, and perhaps a glass of wine."

I knew he'd got the message when he opened the door, wearing nothing but his embossed velvet dressing gown. It curved open entirely, exposing the snail trails on his chest, dark tracings of my desire. Yes, we would dance together. He'd turned our bedroom into a sacred space. The mirror was draped with a woven shawl, and the heady smell of lotus flowers permeated the air. Many candles threw out a soft light over the bed. My heart was in my mouth, but I breathed steadily, pulling my breath down into the nervous energy agitating my pelvis, until I could feel it settle and begin to soften there. As the warmth began to seep up from my sex, into my abdomen and heart, I turned to him.

The body needs to be enlivened to express our awakened passion. Tantric practitioners describe our personal reservoir of Shakti energy as the Kundalini. Like a coiled snake, the Kundalini sleeps at the base of the spine until charmed upward. This dancing exercise mobilizes the spine and pelvis, so that the Kundalini energy can snake up the spine.

By dancing back-to-back in a figure of eight, the Kundalini is awakened; as you dance together, you can imagine the Kundalini energy uncoiling and dancing up your spine, joining with the Kundalini energy of your lover.

Ritual

These movements derive from oriental dancing and feel very natural to the body. While standing, with knees very slightly bent, practice tracing circles with your hips as if you were dancing with a hula hoop, but slowly. Then trace a figure-of-eight, both horizontally and vertically.

Visualize your lover dancing naked on a lotus flower. Imagine this flower is sitting in your heart. Imagine the long green stem of the lotus flower snakes down into your sex.

Feel the warmth of your sexual passion for your lover feeding and nourishing the lotus flower on which he or she sits.

49

CIRCULATING THE ENERGY
OF EJACULATION

 One of the best ways to connect your sexual energy with your heart and your spirituality is to give up your attachment to orgasm. Tantric practitioners believe that focusing on intercourse until you orgasm at the point of ejaculation limits your erotic experience. You lose valuable energy with the ejaculate, which could be used instead to nourish your energy-body.

Particularly for men, ejaculation often means the rapid decline of erotic energy. Try letting go of the drive to orgasm in order to lengthen your pleasure, and focus on the more subtle sensations that make up your sexual pleasure. This practice increases your capacity to sustain arousal without discharging sexual energy through orgasm. Women's ejaculate is not considered depleting; the watery fluids a woman can emit during intense pleasure is considered an ambrosial drink fit for the gods (see page 282).

Learning to extend your sexual pleasure enables you to experience a series of sexual peaks and valleys. You can continue making love for long periods of time in a state of high arousal. You can also experience whole-body orgasms, where the exquisite sensations around your penis spread up and through the rest of your body in waves of energy called streamings. These energy orgasms are delightful, and may or may not be accompanied by ejaculation.

Normal arousal comes in waves, with periods when arousal falls and then climbs again to peaks of excitement. As you do this exercise and your excitement intensifies, focus on breathing through the wave until your excitement drops, without reaching orgasm. Try to back off if you feel yourself coming to the edge of an orgasm, and instead focus on relaxing into the heightened state of arousal and the high levels of erotic energy generated. Relax into your arousal, and slow your breathing rather than allow it to climb and get faster. Keep your movement slow, and breathe deeply in order to avert the approach of orgasm.

Begin by making a joint commitment to delay or avoid ejaculation. If you do inadvertently ejaculate, relax into it and focus on the energy pouring out of the crown of your head.

Ritual

TO THE WOMAN

◆ *Caress your partner's genitals for some time. Lightly brush the pubic hair, gently pull it, and press gently, with different pressures and strokes. Tease the scrotum by cupping the balls and fondling the skin. Tease the lingam (penis) by brushing it with your fingertips and tentatively circling around it.*

◆ *Once your partner is highly aroused and wanting genital stimulation, rub lubricant all over his sexual organs, including the scrotum, perineum and external anus, if he likes being stroked there.*

◆ *Lightly stroke the shaft of his penis and massage the perineum, the area where his penis starts to swell just in front of his anus. Deep massage often feels very pleasurable, so experiment with deep, rhythmic strokes, maintaining the pattern that your partner enjoys. Swap between his penis and perineum to give him waves of pleasure. Stimulating the perineum reduces the drive to ejaculate.*

◆ *Take your partner into this pre-ejaculatory orgasmic state several times, stopping each time he feels he might lose control.*

TO THE MAN

◆ *If you feel you are nearing orgasm, stop moving to avoid further stimulation and squeeze the love muscle to seal energy in your pelvis (see the Love Muscle, page 56, or Retaining the Semen, page 162).*

◆ *Concentrate on dispersing the energy away from your genitals with breathing and visualization. With every in-breath, draw the energy up from your pelvis to the area of your third eye (your brow center), and with your out-breath send this energy out toward your lover. Press the tip of your tongue to the roof of your mouth. Focus pulling your sexual excitement up from your genitals with every inhalation, through the energy channel created by your mouth up to your forehead. Let the energy drop back down to your genitals with your exhalation.*

◆ *At the edge of orgasm, stop. Lie still for half an hour, seeing what happens with this erotic charge. Feel the heightened energy. Allow the erotic feelings to spread throughout your body.*

50

RETAINING THE SEMEN

In order to achieve total control over retention [of semen],
the yogi should contract his anal muscles, draw in his
stomach, and hold his breath while rolling or turning up his
eyes and focusing his mind on the ideal of penetrating
transcendence.

CHANDAMAHAROSANA TANTRA

 Tantric techniques teach you to value an orgasm that
implodes rather than explodes, concentrating rather
than losing vitality. To gain control over your semen emission,
agree a period of time where you will only ejaculate once a
week, trying not to on other occasions when you make love.

Some Tantric practitioners believe that ejaculation depletes
energy, whereas orgasm without ejaculation fills us with nour-

ishment. We are used to thinking about sex as a form of tension release, and most men think that not ejaculating will leave them with sore testicles and feeling dissatisfied.

The key to making semen retention pleasurable seems to be to take your time, not finishing love-making as soon as you feel your testicles becoming distended with semen. Instead you prolong the state of arousal while encouraging the tension in your balls to disperse through breathing and visualization techniques, which concentrate on sending the sexual excitement generated throughout the chakra system. Instead of becoming frustrated, ejaculating less frequently means you can make love more often, for longer periods of time, and your final orgasm is much more intense.

Men's sexual experience is usually divided into the stages of arousal, approach to orgasm, orgasm, and ejaculation. In Tantric sex, these stages are separated. During extended sexual pleasuring men learn to peak and plateau again without going into orgasm. You then learn to orgasm without ejaculation, moving the subtle energies of sexual arousal away from the genitals and up through the inner flute, the central energy channel. By moving energy away from the genitals, ejaculation may subside to be replaced by a whole-body orgasm, in which erotic pleasure and waves of energy spread throughout your body.

> ### BECOMING MULTI-ORGASMIC
>
> *Learning to have more control over when, and how, you reach orgasm means it can become one of a range of erotic possibilities; ejaculation no longer signals the end of love-making, but is just one of the many delightful experiences that are part of sacred sex.*
>
> *If you are able to make love for a long time without coming, you can reach extraordinary states of arousal. Your whole body feels alive and tingling. Some men describe it as a heightened sense of connection with their lover in which they are in a prolonged state of sexual excitement.*

Ritual

It may be easier to try this exercise out when masturbating, at least for the first time you do it. If you get too excited, stop moving and focus on your breathing, rather than the physical sensations.

◆ Stimulate yourself to the very edge of orgasm, when contractions start at the base of your penis, around your prostate and anus. By familiarizing yourself with these sensations, you can learn how to build contractions in intensity in order to orgasm repeatedly without ejaculating.

◆ Take yourself into this pre-ejaculatory orgasmic state several times, and when you have had enough, stop – without having an orgasm. Tell your partner to caress you elsewhere on your body. Focus on your loving feelings for her. Remain still, breathing slowly and deeply.

◆ To lock in your semen, you need to close the seminal vessel coming from the scrotum. Do this by clenching your love muscle, the muscles in the area of your anus and scrotum. Use the mula bhanda (see page 230), locking your anal sphincter. Alternatively, your partner can press your perineum, the area between your scrotum and anus. She presses with all three fingers, applying as much pressure as is comfortable.

◆ Imagine that you are drawing the energy from your perineum up to your heart center, or to the crown of your head, feeling energy streaming up your body.

51

SOLAR-LUNAR BREATHING

 Solar and lunar symbolism is central to Tantra, as they are to many other mystical teachings of both the East and West. The moon is associated with the left side of the body, feminine energy, a cooling quality, the color white, the element of water and the intuitive processes. Lunar energy is stored above the third eye (brow) chakra, and is depicted as a crescent-shaped vessel. The sun is associated with the right side of the body, masculine energy, the element of fire, the color red, and intellect. Solar energy is stored in the solar plexus chakra.

These energies move through two channels which spiral around the central channel, the *sushumna* (see box in radiant energy meditation, page 174). *Ida* carries lunar energy from the left side of the base of the sushumna, crossing over in the forehead and departing through the right nostril. *Pingala* arises on the right side. This solar energy coils round the sushumna before departing through the left nostril.

The following technique consciously unites your solar and lunar breaths. When these are in balance, the life force can travel up the sushumna channel, the "inner flute". The aim of this exercise is to harmonize the energies between you and your partner. The "solar breath" is associated with giving, and the "lunar breath" is associated with receiving. This exercise helps to balance and connect your breathing as a couple. Breath control is used as a means to balance lunar and solar channels. The traditional technique is to breathe through alternate nostrils, using your fingers to block the nostrils. This exercise is adapted from a yoga exercise, *nadi sodhana*, which translates as "clearing the channels". It detoxifies the body and helps energy flow freely through the energy channels. It is deeply relaxing.

Ritual

◆ *Lie on your back, completely relaxed. As you inhale, take your breath down into your hips and relax this area. After several breaths releasing any hip tension, shift your focus to the left hip. Draw your breath down into the left hip, relaxing fully as you breathe out.*

◆ *Take your next breath down into the left leg. Once this is relaxed and heavy, breathe into the left hip, then the* waist, left rib cage, shoulder and then arm, shifting your focus of attention at your own pace. Breathe into the left side of your throat, relaxing as you breathe out. Breathe into the left side of your face and your left brow. Then focus on your genitals.

◆ Switch your focus over to the right side, breathing into the right hip and relaxing it as you breathe out. Breathe into each of the areas of the left side, easing tension with every out-breath until your whole body feels heavy.

◆ For several breaths, focus your mind on the steady flow of air into your body. Imagine the vitality (prana) of the breath nourish your vital force, as you inhale. Breathe at your own pace.

◆ On an exhalation, send your breath from your right brow and down to the right hip. As you inhale, draw the breath back up to the right brow. Breathe in and out as you concentrate on the area in the center of your forehead. On the next exhalation, send your breath down to your left hip. As you breathe in, draw the breath back up to your left brow. Breathe in and out, while concentrating on the energy in the center of your forehead (the area of your third eye, between your eyebrows).

◆ *As you become familiar with sending your breath up and down these energy channels, draw the breath up from one hip with your inhalation and send it down the other side as you exhale, crossing over at the third eye.*

Variation

Try this exercise during love-making. The Tantras suggest that the man consciously draws in the exhaled air from the woman's left nostril through his right nostril, and allows her to consciously breathe in his exhaled breath from the right nostril through her left nostril. Face-to-face lovemaking, with each partner lying on his/her side, facilitates this exchange naturally.

52

•◦•

SUN-MOON MEDITATION

 According to the subtle anatomy mapped by Tantric texts, when women activate their sexual power, they embody the fiery solar energy of the goddess, Shakti, and when men activate their inner wisdom, they embody the meditative consciousness of the god, Shiva, who is known as the "supreme yogi". In this exercise, these two poles can be strengthened and harmonized by meditating on the solar and lunar elements in your own body.

Tantric wisdom says that there is an inner man and an inner woman in each of us. In the man, sperm is concentrated in the brow center, which is ruled by the moon. During love-making, it is alchemically transformed into inner lunar essence, or *soma*, the water of life. When heated by the fire of sexual passion, generated by a woman, or a man's inner woman (the Shakti–Kundalini in his sacrum), this soma overflows, nourishing the whole body with drops of wisdom.

Usually, wisdom is associated with the lunar faculty of feminine intuition, while the solar faculty of power is regarded as a masculine prerogative. However, according to Tantra, women's generative organs are nourished by the inner sun of the navel center.

This exercise utilizes the alchemy of solar and lunar elements in your energy-body for meditation, marrying your own inner man and inner woman. In this way, these opposites join to achieve the ultimate unification of the individual with the divine.

Ritual

You may want to start with the radiant energy meditation (see page 174). Once you have energized your body through meditation, visualize a solar globe in your pelvis, and a crescent moon in your forehead, between your eyebrows. Think of this downward-looking inner moon as a source of nectar that feeds your heart and soul. The nectar, which flows through the subtle channels in your body when the chakra at the crown of your head is activated, nourishes your energy-body.

Variation

While making love, visualize a sun in your pelvis. Let the arousal of your love-making fuel the flames, creating a tremendous heat that radiates from your pelvis. Imagine that in the heat of your love-making this inner fire generates so much heat that it melts the inner moon lying concave over your third eye, so that drops of wisdom drip down over your body. Focus on absorbing the nourishing properties of this ambrosia. It nurtures your faculty of intuition, and generates wisdom.

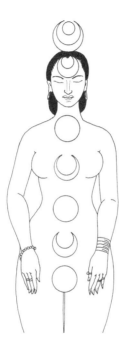

❖

53

RADIANT ENERGY MEDITATION

 Our relationship with the divine is nurtured by regular meditation, prayer, and ritual practice.

This meditation exercise helps you to open the crown center, or chakra (at the top of the head) to connect with divine love. In this practice you can invite the sacred into sex, achieving a sense of union with the divine through union with your beloved.

Ritual

◆ *Sit cross-legged on the floor, facing each other if you are doing this exercise together. Close your eyes and allow your breath to fall into a slow, steady rhythm. This allows you to resonate with each other's body rhythm. Once you have created a calm, tranquil mood, you can add visual imagery to intensify your state of meditation.*

◆ *Visualize opening the crown center at the top of your head, the gateway to the transpersonal realm. Each of you imag-*

ines white light streaming in through the crown of your head. Each time you breathe in, imagine drawing this energy down to the base of your pelvis. As the energy fills your pelvis, hold your breath for a moment, allowing it to permeate your being. Try to imagine this stream of white light expanding out to fill your whole being, illuminating your body so that it becomes a radiant energy-body.

◆ Release your breath slowly, while your energy-body remains illuminated by your breath.

◆ Focus on the sexual energy in your genitals, allowing the white light to concentrate in your pelvis. Imagine that you are drawing this golden light from your genitals and pelvis with your breath, along the column through the center of your body. As it moves up toward the crown of your head again, imagine this golden light flooding the energy centers located at your heart, your throat, and your brow (third eye). Then visualize the light streaming out of your crown, to merge with the light streaming out of your partner's head.

◆ Visualize the energy streaming out of the crown of both your heads pooling and uniting. See yourselves as radiant beings surrounded in a rainbow of light, linked to the divine.

THE PATH OF GRACE

The central energy channel of the body is called the sushumna, otherwise known as the great axis. Sushumna means "the most gracious", the direct path of grace. Through it, the body can receive divine energy. The central channel is rooted at the base of the spine and climbs up along the spinal chord and out the crown of the head, linking the microcosm of the body with the macrocosm of the universe. This channel transmits energy as it awakens from its sleep at the base of the spine.

Variation

You can use the energy meditation while making love. Sit in the Shiva–Shakti position where the woman sits in the man's lap with his erect penis inside.

54

CONNECTING WITH ECSTASY: BECOMING THE DIVINE COUPLE

Bliss is my very nature

I need not do anything nor strive for anything to secure it.

Bliss follows me wherever I go

It is more real to me than my body,

It is nearer to me than my mind.

Happiness that is dependent on something is only another

form of misery.

A RISHI'S PERSPECTIVE, AS QUOTED BY DEEPAK CHOPRA

 The Tantric concept of unity through attaining oneness with the divine is often expressed as Shakti–Shiva, a unification of both energy and consciousness. In sexual rapture, two bodies and souls merge into one.

Tantrics depict this unification as the great goddess, Shakti, and her consort, Shiva, together in sexual ecstasy, representing the indivisibility of energy and consciousness.

In Tantra's creation myth, from Shakti and Shiva's ecstatic union a golden nectar rains down, bathing the world in bliss. This nectar, amrita, nourishes all of creation, and tastes of pure joy.

When we are in harmony with the true nature of reality we experience it as an integration of being, consciousness, and bliss. This is called "love". This altered state of awareness is what Tantrics mean by "religious experience".

Making love as if you are the divine couple reinstates bliss as your birthright. In this exercise, you invite the presence of Shiva and Shakti into your love-making, participating in their primal bliss by letting the divine lovers make love through your bodies.

Ritual

◆ *Set up a sacred space by arranging a temple of love for your love-making (see page 38).*

◆ *Honor your partner as divine, and crown each other with the gift of a flower garland.*

◆ *Make love as if you were a god and goddess. Once you are both highly aroused by non-penetrative sex, take up the Shiva–Shakti position (woman sitting on the man, who is sitting cross-legged on the floor, supported by cushions). As always in Tantric love-making, the woman chooses the appropriate moment to guide her partner's lingam (penis) inside her. Once her yoni is moist and juicy, she receives his lingam as an instrument of dynamic male energy. He enters her yoni as the source of creative female energy. Simultaneously, visualize your energy bodies interpenetrating.*

◆ *While making love, visualize the divine lovers embracing above you and imagine their spiritual emanations enveloping you in a state of grace.*

55

⋅►◄⋅

SHIVA MEDITATION

Ever gracious, ever blissful Lord [Shiva], whose compassion is
like an ocean of nectar
Your body shines white as the jasmine flower.
Purest truth, robed in space, omnipresent, loving and
beloved lord of yogis.

MAHANIRVANA TANTRA

In Hindu mythology, Shiva was the lord of creation,
who danced the whole universe into existence. Another version says that the universe was created during a bout
of love-making lasting an eternity. The seed that poured from
his erect lingam (phallus) brought the whole world into being.

In this exercise, you identify with the omnipotence and
creativity of Shiva, who stands for transcendent masculinity,

so becoming a more than mortal man. Shiva is considered the supreme yoga practitioner – a master of meditation. Use this dynamic meditation to explore your potency and creative wisdom. Or, you can use it to demonstrate your prowess to your beloved; she could lead you through this meditation, prompting you whenever appropriate.

Ritual

First, find some atmospheric music to help you get in the mood for dancing the dance of creation.

◆ *Stand with your eyes closed, locating yourself as all alone in the void. There is nothing around you but darkness. Feel what it is like to be in this emptiness, this infinite spaciousness. Really experience the emptiness – this is the fundamental nature of existence underneath all the phenomenal drama of our lives. Sense the neutral, non-threatening quality of emptiness; it just is.*

◆ *Express this feeling in your dance. Use your arms to express the sense of spaciousness, and your body to respond to the void.*

◆ *Become aware of your breath in the void. Feel all the*

energy of space passing through you with every inhalation and exhalation.

◆ *Shift your awareness to yourself, and use your body and arms to expand your sense of yourself and fill up the surrounding space. Spread out into the cosmos. You are the god Shiva, lord of creation. Send your creative energy throughout infinite space. Enjoy the sensations of your body as you drum up energy and transmit it, using gestures.*

◆ *Become aware of the sensuality of your being. Touch your skin if you like, becoming aware of the pleasure of existence. Abandon yourself to the pleasure of your improvized dance. You are dancing for yourself – as if there is no-one else present. Enjoy your sensuality for its own sake.*

◆ *From the excitement generated by your dance, imagine your penis quickening. Let it expand, full of the potential of your own creativity. See it blazing like fire with the heat generated through excitement and visualize light pouring out of your penis, lighting up the space around.*

◆ *See yourself clearly now, illuminated by the light you have generated. You are the god Shiva, potent lord of creation. Imagine yourself scattering your semen, bestowing it throughout the reaches of the universe. As your seed flies*

through space, it becomes galaxies. You are creating whole worlds with your seed. See the nebulae, the stars, the planets, the moon, as the fruit of your loins.

◆ *As you scatter your seed, whole continents spring up, and vast oceans. Visualize mountain ranges, forests and rivers spring up as your arms distribute your plenty. Your largesse creates plant life, fish, and animals. In your mind's eye, see the bees and tigers, ants and elephants falling from your hands. You are creating every kind of species; one of each, male and female.*

◆ *Once you have created everything, look in your mind's eye in wonder at your own handiwork. Feel the awesomeness of creation, and dance to celebrate its beauty. Celebrate the universe you have created as a god. Celebrate your own power. Lose yourself in the dance.*

His desire for me was enough for both of us. His seed would fill me, permeating every cell of my body, pushing me out of my limited, earthbound body. From his seed I could draw my sustenance, sucking it into me, making it mine, making my desire grow, turning his desire into mine … making our desire bigger than both of us.

‒•◆•‒

56

WORSHIP YOUR PARTNER'S SEX

The phallus of Shiva is erect because it is raised to full consciousness, and in full consciousness it penetrates the universe. The vulva of Shakti is open because in full consciousness she lets the universe penetrate her …
At the core of their mutual penetration supreme consciousness reins.

FROM *TANTRIC QUEST*, DANIEL ODIER

 The Shiva principle of consciousness is particularly concentrated in men, but every woman also embodies Shiva energies. The symbol of Shiva is a lingam, an erect phallus that represents the creator.

Your lover's lingam is a source of your pleasure. For him it represents his masculinity, and when he feels good about this

his sexual confidence increases. Treating his genitals with reverence also reminds you both of their sacredness.

Although Tantric art represents the lingam as erect, the aim of this exercise is to honor your partner's penis in its natural, relaxed state. This allows him to experience his lingam in a non-sexual way – neither as an instrument he should be ready to use, nor as a source of ambivalence or shame. Your intention is very important here, and it is essential not to step over the boundaries of the exercise so that Shiva can really let go and receive your devotion.

Ritual

◆ *With your partner sitting with his legs wide open, leaning back on some comfortable cushions and gazing at you, kneel before his lingam, and bow before it, presenting your gift. Offer his lingam long white flowers such as lilies, saying "I offer you these flowers, charged with my love, devotion, and erotic energy."*

◆ *Then make a garland to garland your partner with by threading each flower through the stem of the one before – just as you fashioned daisy chains as a child. For larger flowers you can thread them together with gardening wire.*

- *Gaze at his lingam, taking time to really look, and then tell your partner what you see, and what you like about what you see. Really take in how his lingam looks, and gaze in your partner's eyes when you tell him. Drip a few drops of clear water over your partner's lingam, worshipping him as the god Shiva.*

- *When he invites you to touch his lingam, use a gentle and reverential touch. You're not aiming to excite him, but to explore him. Stroke his pubic area, his scrotum, his perineum, and his lingam.*

- *Explore different touches. Use a light touch, especially around the scrotum, and hold his balls delicately, as if they were eggs. Stroke and massage the sensitive skin of the testicles, blow on the delicate skin around the testicles and perineum – then try taking his scrotum into your mouth.*

- *Finger the shaft of your partner's lingam as if it were a flute. Travel around the lingam, avoiding the usual up and down stroking that mimics intercourse. You are not aiming to excite and bring your partner to orgasm. You are both focussing on the importance of his lingam and the masculine energy that is so important to your relationship.*

LINGAM AND YONI AS ENERGY

Lingam is the Sanskrit term for phallus, and it is always depicted erect. It stands for the world in a state of excitement – in response to the tantalizing play of dynamic Shakti energy. Graphic images and sculptured representations of genitals are worshipped as symbols for the female and male energies that together make up existence. In Tantra, the lingam stands for focused awareness and the transcendent, masculine consciousness of Shiva, the integration of the carnal realm, and the retention of semen in ritual sex. Both genitals are complementary and connected. Just as Shakti and Shiva are always entwined, so too are the yoni and lingam, represented all over India by carved yoni-lingam sculptures, representing a phallus arising out of a vulva.

57

❖

HONORING YONI

Yoni means vulva. A woman's genitals represent Shakti energy, because this is where primordial female energy is the most concentrated. The Sanskrit word also refers to a sacred space or sanctum and in Tantra, the genitals are worshipped with love and respect, as is the phallus.

In Western culture, genitals are often seen as dirty, and women's genitals particularly have been degraded. The aim of this exercise is to turn this around, learning to appreciate your partner's genitals, and revere them as the source of bliss. Honor your lover as the fount of creation and sexuality.

Ritual

Bring a gift or offering to present to your partner's yoni; it could be a flower or a shell whose shape reminds you of her labia, or it could be something that would remind your partner of her own vulva.

- *Start with a namaste (see page 2)*
- *Make your partner comfortable on some cushions, with her knees spread apart. Kneel before her yoni and bow, then present your gift.*
- *Offer red roses or rose petals to your partner's yoni, worshipping her. Say "I give you these flowers, as symbol of my devotion to your sexuality. I honor your sex as the origin of all creative energy."*
- *Look at her yoni with reverence and wonder. For the woman, it can be a profound experience. Many women are uncomfortable when their genitals are exposed, even when used to plenty of oral sex. Look at your partner with reverence and wonder. It's important for her to see the love in your eyes.*
- *Gaze at her yoni for some time, absorbing her genitals through your eyes. Then tell her what you like, while looking into her eyes.*
- *If your partner wishes, she invites you to touch her yoni. Your touch should be extremely gentle and reverential. Explore her vulva rather than exciting her. Concentrate on the textures of different parts of her yoni: the pubic hair, the inner and outer lips, her pearl (clitoris), vaginal*

entrance, perineum (toward the anus), and rosetta (anus).
She can give you feedback on how you are touching her.

◆ *Kiss and lick her yoni. While you do this, concentrate on*
absorbing the essence of her yoni, rather than arousing
her. She relaxes and enjoys receiving your attention with-
out feeling she should or shouldn't get aroused. Again,
experience what this feels like, and really taste and smell
the different parts of her yoni.

◆ *Finish by gently laying your hand, palm down, against her*
pubic mound, to honor her sex.

SHAKTI THE DIVINE

Shakti refers to the divine feminine creative energy that pervades
the whole of existence. In Tantra, Shakti is revered as the active
principle, out of which consciousness (the Shiva principle)
emerges. Shakti is as changeable as the phenomenal world she
has brought into being.

58

WORSHIPPING KALI: INITIATION INTO LOVE'S MYSTERIES

Kali gave to woman total sexuality, the capacity for infinite pleasure. In doing so, Kali bestowed on woman the ability to control all parts of her body for her own pleasure and that of her mate. Female pleasure is the seat of all pleasure. In developing her body's capacity for pleasure, so shall she bring forth the ability to give pleasure.

FROM *TANTRA, THE KEY TO SEXUAL POWER AND PLEASURE*

For women to access sexual pleasure, complete abandon is required. Once you have discovered what arouses you, let go of your inhibitions. Give in to your erotic sensations and let yourself rest in the sensations of lightness and floating that come with sexual pleasure. Too much effort – trying to make yourself come – makes you tense and reduces your sensuality.

In this exercise, the longing for release pushes you to explore and search. Use your longing to power your search for liberation through sexuality. For tonight, you are in charge; make love in all the ways that suit you, at the pace you enjoy, and ask your lover for whatever you want, whenever you want it. Don't be reluctant to change pace or change the mood – just explore your own desires, and own your pleasure fully. When you feel sure of your sexuality you can confidently explore your eroticism in the spirit of playful adventure without insecurity or guilt. Draw on your own erotic power to confer sexual power on your lover. In Tantra, women are considered initiators into the mysteries of love.

Ritual

◆ *Start with a meditation to access your sexual confidence. Focus on your inherent wisdom – energy, sexual knowledge, intuition, sensitivity, spontaneity, playfulness, joy, and pleasure. See yourself brimming with these qualities in your inner eye. Bask in your own power.*

♦ *Then confidently invite your lover to participate in mystical experience with you. Drink a glass of wine together, toasting your inner goddess. Move to his left side, the side associated with active, initiatory power. Feel your power emanating from you.*

♦ *He speaks your name as a mantra, repeating it over and over again while winding a red silk scarf around your hips. He can make up a song celebrating your virtues and sing as he adorns your body. Take in his adoration of you.*

♦ *Dance sensuously for your lover, feeling your own seductive power (see page 206). You may want some rhythmic music to help immerse yourself in your own voluptuousness and the potency of your sexual charisma.*

♦ *When you feel full of the sensual pleasure of your own movements, squat on your heels, legs open to reveal your sex. Invite your lover to worship your yoni as the source of pleasure and creativity (see page 190). Display your genitals with pride.*

♦ *Invite him to touch your thighs and waist, approaching your yoni with a gentle touch. Guide his hands as and where you want them (see pages 50 and 248). Take charge of this night of love-making.*

◆ *Give in to your desire and pleasure. Your partner's role is to hold back on his own pleasure and facilitate you in exploring your desires, in whatever way you wish. Use movement, breathing, and the exact sexual postures that you prefer to fully focus on experiencing your own pleasure. Explore positions for intercourse where you straddle your lover, giving you control over the depth, pace, and rhythm of movement of his penis. Enjoy!!*

KALI

The goddess Kali represents the voracious, lustful and dominating power of feminine sexuality. In Tantric rituals, her role is of sexual initiator – a woman who teaches sexual secrets to her lover. In Tantric cosmology, the feminine principle is active, and the male is conscious. In this exercise you explore feminine sexuality as active and directive, while masculine consciousness is as a witness, being fully present and responsive.

59

OPENING YOUR HEART

 During meditation, it is particularly important to increase awareness of the heart area. Once this energy center has been balanced, it will harmonize the others. The lotus symbolizes spiritual awakening, because of its delicate petals and how they open to reveal a perfect flower. The stalk is nourished by mud (representing the mire of daily life). Tantrics use it as a symbol of creation, which supports all the manifest phenomena in the world. It also represents the female genitals, the yoni, the source of man's creation. The three relationship arenas of erotic attraction, emotional connection, and intellectual compatibility need to be imbued with your open-hearted love for each other. This heart meditation exercise helps you create a deeper realization of your love.

Ritual

◆ *Sit cross-legged, facing each other with knees touching. Let your hands rest over your knees. Have your right hand upturned, so that your partner can lay the palm of their left hand upon it. This creates a link between your two energy bodies.*

◆ *Close your eyes. Still your mind and concentrate on your breathing, allowing it to become slow, regular, and in time together.*

◆ *When you have dropped into a state of relaxation, focus on the area of your chest between your breasts, called the heart center. Imagine a lovely lotus sitting in your heart, a bowl of creamy white petals tinged with pink. As you breathe in, imagine these petals opening outward, closing again with each gentle exhalation. Imagine them gradually opening further with each gentle pulse of your breath. As the lotus opens, let the glory of it fill your heart with love.*

◆ *Visualize your partner and place them sitting in the middle of this lotus in your heart, surrounded by love. Imagine this for several minutes.*

◆ *Then, with every out-breath, let your love travel down your right arm, into the heart of your partner. With every*

in-breath, receive the loving energy they send down their
arm from the lotus in their heart.

Variation

While doing this meditation, sit with your right hand cupped
over your lover's heart, and your left hand resting on your knee
with your thumb and index finger touching at the tip. This
mudra is a power form, which creates a flowing energy circuit
in your body.

60

CREATING A DREAM BODY

 In this exercise, you use a yoga technique, nidra yoga, to access your higher consciousness and influence your dreams. This involves using auto-suggestion at the moment of transition between consciousness and sleep. You can use it to dream of your beloved and to ask for higher spiritual guidance for your relationship. In Tantric terms, you are creating a relationship body in the imaginal realm when you both do this technique together.

The moment of transition is known as bindu, when images and free-floating thoughts wander through your awareness without any effort or concern on the part of your conscious mind. This time of transition between waking and sleeping is when your unconscious is receptive to any auto-suggestions you wish to make.

Ritual

◆ *Before you go to sleep, lie with your partner in a spoon shape (see page 236). Let your breath fall into a slow, gentle pattern. Inhale, drawing your breath in through your pelvis, and exhale through your mouth.*

◆ *Synchronize the rate of your breathing first, then focus attention on your energy centers, or chakras. Both of you start breathing in and out through your sexual center into the base of your spine so that you are breathing in through your genitals together and out through your mouth, to harmonize your base chakra with that of your partner. After several breaths, move the breath up to your sexual center, drawing your inhalation into this area simultaneously. Go through each chakra in turn, tuning it with your breath by drawing the breath upwards into this area and down and out through your genitals (see page xv for chakra map).*

◆ *Once you have tuned all your chakras together, imagine you are both lying in an ocean of ambrosia. In the middle of the ocean lies a fertile island of rose quartz. You can see trees laden with sweet-smelling flowers and lotuses filling the waterways. In the forest is a tree known as the wish-*

fulfilling tree, whose branches represent knowledge and wisdom. In the branches is a tree-platform, surrounded by amazing gems. The light glints off the fabulous stones, creating a rainbow of colors. Imagine you and your beloved are lying on the platform. Embrace and prepare for sleep.

◆ *As you enter sleep, in your visualization and in reality, take a moment to invite your lover into your dreams. Visualize your lover in your brow chakra, the center of vision located between your eyes (sometimes called the third eye), and offer up the request for a dream to the wish-fulfilling tree. Inwardly state, "I am ready to receive a dream to guide us in our relationship."*

◆ *In the morning, share your dreams with your lover. Describe how your lover appears in your dream, and the mood evoked by their presence. Discuss any striking figure who appears in your dreams, to see whether they may represent the wisdom of your relationship.*

◆ *You may need to practice this technique several times before accessing your higher consciousness, therefore it is good to get into the habit of sharing your dreams.*

205

61

TEMPLE DANCE

Visualize yourself as an erotic red goddess;
symbol of dedication and passion.
Three eyes blazing with passion;
your tongue is lustful, with the purifying power
of your inner fire.
You are a naked goddess, with disheveled hair;
symbolizing freedom from the bonds of delusion.
You are intuition – a reminder that everything must pass.
Blazing like a fire you express your wisdom essence,
in embracing your lover without restraint.

CHAKRA SAMBHARA TANTRA

 In India, temple dancers were dedicated to the great
goddess, and their dances were performed in honor

and praise of her. Dance was seen as a form of meditation or prayer. Centuries ago, these dancers initiated men into sacred sex in temple precincts, before their arts became demeaned as prostitution.

This ritual allows you to physically embody your erotic energy through dance, and offer it for your partner's pleasure. Just as there are many different aspects of deity, represented in Tantra by different goddesses and gods, so you can enjoy exploring different moods and aspects of yourself. Everyone has feminine and masculine aspects, so you can dance as either Shakti or Shiva, her consort. Your dance can be seductive or playful, reverential or meditative according to your mood.

Ritual

As you prepare, think about your intention to celebrate your intrinsic beauty and self-worth through dance. Wear something comfortable that makes you feel beautiful – or perhaps just a silky scarf. Choose your favorite music to dance in your own unique style for your partner – for at least a quarter of an hour.

Your partner waits in expectation, feeling honored that you will dance as a goddess. Start the dance with a salutation

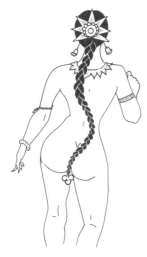

to your partner, who sits on a cushion watching you appreciatively. Don't worry about pleasing them. They will enjoy your pleasure or abandonment in the dance.

Choose some fast, dynamic music that encourages you to overcome your inhibitions and feel energized. Stand up with your feet a comfortable distance apart, bend your knees slightly, and start by shaking your hips to loosen up and awaken your energy. Shake your whole body, getting rid of tension and tightness wherever you feel it.

Now that your body is relaxed and loosened up, start to dance. Play any music that you enjoy, and let yourself go, expressing yourself without inhibition.

When you've finished, ask your partner to dance for you while you take your place on the cushions.

I luxuriated in the sight. Lying back on a heap of cushions I felt like a choreographer, watching my lead dancer enact what had until then been a creative dream. He opened the dance with tentative, coy gestures, inviting my sympathy. Then, feeling more confident, he surprised me with his gestures and his stamping feet. Sometimes charming, sometimes powerfully overwhelming, the masculinity of his dance was like nothing I'd known or seen before. It was so different from my own self-contained yet seductive undulations.

He beckoned me with his eyes, drawing me toward his sweating body. As his smell curled into my nostrils he pulled away, tantalizing me to follow him.

A low, steady drumbeat summoned me. The drumbeats crept up my spine. My spine was dancing to their syncopated rhythms. I joined him in the dance, as we gazed into each other's eyes.

62

•◆•

FIRE BREATH

He didn't touch me, take my hand, or brush against me as
we moved silently through the temple, but I could feel an
invisible energy connecting us. We stood before the yoni-
lingam, when he turned and gazed at me for a long time. His
look was so piercing, yet soft and gentle, like a caress over
my forehead and across my cheeks. As he gazed, every part
of me felt caressed by a feather-like breath, as though the
warm scent of his breath stroked me. My nipples felt hot and
cold and I could feel a line of tingling from my navel to
between my breasts.

A heat began in my vagina, glowing like a half extinguished
ember from the night before. His breath was fanning the
embers in my vulva, and I felt my whole vulva warm and full.
I wanted to dance around his lingam in spirals and figure
eight, the way the serpent coiled around the lingam before

us. I took a few deep breaths and felt the heat in my sex spreading up my navel and buttocks leaving a warm glow.

He was waiting for me, but not here … not in the temple. We would create our own sacred space from our need and desire. I reached for his hand. It was like an electric shock, the charge between us was so great that touching produced a great jolt of energy. But my hand stayed around his, and I drew him to the low door of the temple.

We found a path leading from the dusty courtyard behind some huts, toward terraced fields. There behind the lip of a disused terrace I folded him into my arms, melting around him. I could feel the warmth of his chest through his fine cotton shirt. His heart followed my heart, a syncopated call and response to each other until we fell into one rhythm, two hearts beating as one.

This breathing technique uses the fast pumping of the diaphragm to enable you to breath rapidly and vigorously. It is used as a form of purification, and you can try it whenever you feel full of emotions, which need to be cleared before love-making.

Ritual

◆ *Sit comfortably, with your neck and shoulders relaxed. If there is any tension there, loosen up by massaging each other's shoulders. If you're on your own, loosen up by rotating your arms like windmills while standing up. If your neck is stiff, rest your chin on your chest, relaxing your neck totally and then gently rolling it right around over your shoulder and backwards, before coming back the other side.*

◆ *Start by using this variation of the complete breath technique (see page 10): make your exhalation last twice as long as your inhalation, and try to hold your breath for four times' the duration of the in-breath. For example: inhale for two counts, hold for eight counts, and slowly exhale for four counts.*

◆ *After several rounds of this, you can start the rapid exhalation that turns your breathing into the breath of fire. Don't worry about the in-breath – because you've forced your oxygen out by suddenly pulling in your abdominal*

muscles, you will automatically take a breath to replenish the oxygen. This rapid series of contractions and release will get prana, vital energy, moving through you.

Variation

You can try this breathing technique using Frank Natale's meditation tape, *Fire Breath*, available in the UK.

63
·◆·

UNITING HEAVEN AND
EARTH MEDITATION

Diamond Light Tantra teacher Leora Lightwoman uses this meditation to unify the red energy of passion with the white energy of spirituality, described by Tantrics as solar and lunar elements. It links the sensual world with the world of spirit, connecting the erotic and the divine in your relationship.

This connection is essential to nourish and awaken the chakras located in your heart, throat and head. You nourish them by using the raw primal power of your sexual desire to foster ever deepening levels of intimacy. One person can guide their partner (slowly reading the text to them), or it can be used as a solo meditation.

Ritual

You may want to tape this meditation so that you can both follow it together.

◆ *Sit comfortably with a straight back. Imagine that you are growing roots down into the ground, through the soles of your feet (or from the base of your spine, if you are sitting cross-legged). These energetic roots reach deep into the earth.*

◆ *As you breathe in and out, imagine these roots expanding and growing, until they reach through the layers of earth toward the earth's core. With each out-breath, send your roots deeper and deeper, until they near the molten lava at the center of the earth. Feel the intense heat as you contact the hot, fiery core of the earth, symbolizing your connection to the source of life. Feel the energy that this brings you.*

◆ *As you continue to breathe, draw up this heat and redness, this source of life and energy. It is your own passion, your lust for life, and your desire to be alive, here and now. Keep breathing and drawing this energy up through your roots, right into the soles of your feet. Feel the heat, or imagine its there, right under the soles of your feet.*

◆ *As you breathe in, allow the warmth to spread up your legs and into your pelvis. Draw that red-hot energy into your sexual organs. Allow the heat to burn away anything* that interferes with your love of life, with joy, with vibrancy. Breathe in, drawing that heat into your abdomen. Imagine it burning away any obstacles to your passion and vitality.

◆ Then draw that energy into your lungs and chest, allowing your lungs to expand with the fullness of life. Breathe in, drawing passion into the center of your chest, in the area of your heart. Feel your heart expand as it fills with breath, and become warm with your ardor for life and love. Allow the fire to burn away any problems with love.

◆ Pull the energy into the crown area at the top of your head. Imagine that you are sprouting branches, a crown that reaches up into the sky. Feel these energetic channels reaching into the cool white fire of the universe – the realm beyond mortal life, of the infinite, and of spirit.

◆ Absorb the cool white fire of spirituality through the branches into the crown at the top of your head. Focus on opening up your crown area, to allow the cool white fire of the universe to rain down on your head like sparks. Feel the sense of infinite possibilities for you, of spaciousness, and expansion.

◆ *Bring this sense of spaciousness into your chest. Let your heart be soothed by it, releasing emotions of being wounded or armored. Imagine the cool white fire of the heavens burning together with the hot red fire of earth in your heart, mixing and mingling in the heat. See your heart as the bridge between heaven and earth. Celebrate the roots that connect you to the earth, your body and the material world, and the branches that connect you to the world of spirit.*

◆ *As you breathe out, let the energy of this red and white heat expand, filling your heart with love. Send your love toward your partner, and let it flow from your partner to the whole world beyond. As you breathe out, imagine love flowing out of you. As you breathe in, imagine receiving love. Breathe in and out, receiving and giving love.*

64

ANOINTING THE CHAKRAS

Her cool fingers circulated the air above my sacrum, combing and dragging it as if my body was extruding tentacles of sticky muck that needed cleaning. Unbidden, I felt desire stir as she decontaminated my energy field.

Her hand hovered over my genital area, and I felt a lot of cool air moving under her palm. As her hands moved up to my navel, I realized she was energizing each chakra. The cool air moving over the solar plexus began to warm. I opened my eyes to see her leaning over me, sending all her energy into the area of my heart. I wanted to smile at her, to make contact from the distant place I had dropped into, but she didn't respond. I allowed myself to drop back down into a state of deep relaxation, receiving the energy she stimulated.

In this ritual, you map the energy-body of your beloved by anointing his or her chakras, or energy centers, activating them with oils.

You will need seven essential oils. If you're familiar with their qualities, use those that you associate with each chakra. Otherwise, try ylang-ylang for the base (root) chakra; sage for the navel; eucalyptus for the solar plexus; rose for the heart; mint for the throat; and lavender, or a combination oil of your choice, for the crown chakra. Always dilute essential oils in a base oil, such as almond, before applying to the skin. Add several drops of the essential oil (just enough to appreciate the aroma) to the almond oil base.

Ritual

To start, make a comfortable nest with a duvet and cushions and ask your partner to lay down there naked.

◆ *For the base (root) chakra: Kneeling beside your beloved, first inhale the diluted ylang-ylang essential oil. Inhale to absorb the aroma and breathe the smell down into your own root chakra (between your legs). Your partner can watch you, visualizing the movement of energy from your mouth down into the area of your base chakra. Using imagination helps to harmonize both your chakras at the same time. Next, reverentially waft the bottle of undiluted essential oil under your partner's nose, allowing him or her to absorb this smell. As they inhale the odor down into the base chakra, lightly place dilute essential oil at the area of the base chakra (rub a drop on the area covered by pubic hair).*

◆ *For the sexual chakra: Inhale the sage essential oil, drawing the smell sensation from your nose and lungs into your second chakra, while your beloved gazes into your eyes and shares this process. As you anoint the energy center located in their navel with the dilute sage oil, they focus on drawing their breath into that chakra and filling it with creative energy.*

◆ *For the solar plexus chakra: Place a tiny amount of diluted eucalyptus on the tip of your finger; the scent is strong and can be*

overpowering. Keep your finger at some distance from your partner's nose, so it doesn't overpower the smell sensations to follow. Then rub it into the area of the solar plexus. As it penetrates the solar plexus, the person lying down imagines a deep warmth emanating from this area, permeating the whole body.

◆ *For the heart chakra: waft essence of rose under your partner's nose before applying it liberally to their chest, between the breasts. Both of you, feel your heart open like a rose.*

◆ *For the throat chakra: Waft mint essential oil briefly before your lover and then apply it, dilute, to the throat, invigorating that area. Use mint to stimulate the chakra, while your lover imagines it opening the inner eye.*

◆ *For the crown chakra: Anoint the crown chakra at the top of the head with lavender. Your lover can relax into the soothing quality of this essential oil.*

65

HONOR YOUR BODY AS A TEMPLE

Shakti, your body is the world.
The rivers are your veins,
And the forest, your hair.
The firmament is your dress.
The mind is your breath.
You are the pairs of opposites,
You are the past and the present,
The soft and the gentle,
The terrible and the fierce,
Your sounds are silence,
You are the waves of sound,
And the power of silence,
You are the human and the Divine.
You are elevated places,
The labyrinth,
The one without a second.
O Mother of many aspects.

FROM *MANTRAS: WORDS OF POWER BY SWAMI SIVANANDA RADHA*

Honor the goddess by inviting her presence into the temple of your body. The great goddess is the guardian of love, and in worshiping her, you honor love. In this ritual, you acknowledge her presence in the body of your beloved.

Traditionally, you charge your own body or the body of your lover by visualizing deities in these locations. Each chakra, or energy center, is associated with a specific deity; for example, Ganesh, the elephant god, is connected with the root or base chakra. In the Tibetan Tantric tradition, the green Tara, goddess of compassion, is associated with the heart center. This method of energizing the body of your lover is called *nyasa*, or "placement".

Ritual

This exercise uses flowers. Choose seven lovely flowers to place on each of the seven chakras. Those listed here are merely suggestions. Choose those that appeal to you both.

◆ *Red for the root (base) chakra: red dahlia*
◆ *Orange for the sexual chakra: tiger lily*
◆ *Yellow for the solar plexus chakra: sunflower*

- *Pink for the heart chakra: pink rose (emerald green is also associated with the heart, especially in the Tibetan tradition)*
- *Blue for the throat chakra: cornflower*
- *Violet for the brow (third eye) chakra: iris*
- *White for the crown chakra: passionflower*

Variation

Instead of using cut flowers, you can visualize a lotus flower on each of your body chakras (see page 218). You can lie down alone and do this, or simultaneously visualize the appropriate colours in the chakras with your partner.

SHAKTI TEMPLES

Your body is a representation of the divine, just as temples are architectural representations of the divine realm. Temples evolved from simple buildings into more grandiose structures, with a series of halls leading to the inner sanctum (womb chamber) of the temple's principal deity. According to an ancient transformation myth appreciated by Tantrics, parts of Shakti's body fell to the ground. Temples were built where her yoni (genitals), nipples, tongue, and other body parts landed, and these sites are still actively worshipped in India today.

66

DESIGN, CREATE, AND MEDITATE
ON A YANTRA

In traditional Tantra, meditating on yantras, and chanting mantras are used as ways of focusing the mind, and so creating a ritual intention. This enables your energy to flow more smoothly in ways that you want it to. Meditating on a yantra – and the physical act of creating a yantra design – helps align your personal energy with the energy that Tantrics call Shakti-Kundalini.

A yantra is a power form, just as mantras are power words. Yantras are a simple form of mandala. The dot in the center is called a *bindu*, or energy spot. It represents the focal point of creation, which is the source of the yantra's power. Ritual sexual postures are also called yantras, because they create an energy field by aligning the energy centers in the body. As an enclosed sacred space, the term is often used to refer to the yoni, or vagina.

This yantra exercise helps women own their sexual power, and it helps men harmonize their personal power with the sexual energy of the universe.

The yantra here is dedicated to the goddess, Kali. In Tantric rituals, yantras are used to represent a deity by literally standing in for their presence.

Ritual

You can use rice, sand, or any other material to trace the design on the floor, or on large sheets of paper. You can also paint one with poster paints or any other medium with which you are familiar. As you make it, focus on the deity it represents. Your body is your personal yantra. Meditate on your own body as a sacred energy map, or that of your lover.

◆ *Draw a large circle with eight lotus petals around it.*

◆ *As you draw the lotus leaves, focus on the loving feelings in your heart.*

◆ *Next, draw the surrounding square with a "temple gate" on each side.*

◆ *Then, draw five downward-pointing triangles, each one inside the previous triangle, getting smaller and smaller.*

◆ *As you draw the five triangles, focus your mind on the yoni.*

◆ *Finally, draw the red spot, known as bindu, in the center of the smallest triangle.*

◆ *As you draw the red spot, or bindu, focus on the Shakti Kundalini energy in the base of your spine.*

◆ *Gaze at the yantra for several minutes in meditation.*

Open yourself up to the divine qualities of Kali (see page 194). Meditate on the yantra to nourish your personal energy with the source of sexual energy in the universe.

THE SHRI YANTRA

The Shri yantra is dedicated to the goddess, Tripura Sundani. The design is made of five downward-pointing triangles, which represent Shakti (feminine) energy, and four upward-pointing triangles, which symbolize Shiva (masculine) energy. This gives nine triangles, which is a sacred number. In Tantra the number three corresponds to three fundamental principles of creation; immanence, transcendence and integration. The number nine, being comprised of three sets of three, potentizes this triad. The shri chakra contains nine mutually penetrating triangles. These triangles converge on a central energy point, the bindu, representing Shakti, the ultimate source of creative power.

67

BUILDING SEXUAL ENERGY WITH MUDRAS: SACRED GESTURES OF LOVE

 Mudra refers to a ritual gesture in devotional worship in which the hands invoke the presence of a deity. Mudra also refers to the female partner in Tantric practices of sacred sex as well as muscular seals to contain energies in the body, which help the practitioner identify with the deity.

The Yoni mudra is a classic hand gesture for the goddess, in which the fingers are interlaced with each other. There are seals for producing *amrita*, the ambrosial nectar of bliss, and others for enhancing meditation states. For instance, the Seal of Wisdom is used while sitting in the lotus, or hero, posture for meditation, to focus and concentrate the mind. The Anjali mudra, or "seal of honoring", is used to welcome a divine presence. This gesture, in which the hands are pressed together in prayer, is used in the Hindu form of greeting, namaste (see page 2).

This exercise seals energy at the root center and throat

center, allowing you to build up erotic energy between these two points in your energy-body. It is based on a traditional technique called the mula bhanda, which is used to contain sexual energies within the body so they can be circulated. The exercise raises sexual energy within the closed energy circuit created by the seals.

For this practice, you will need to squeeze the pubococcygeal muscles, or love muscle (see page 56) with slow, deep breathing. To practice lengthening your breath, slowly inhale to the count of ten, hold for ten, and slowly exhale for ten. Practice this slow breathing technique daily at least a hundred times to improve your lung capacity (see page 10), if your breathing is fast and shallow. Once you can vary your breathing rate comfortably you are ready to start this exercise.

Ritual

◆ *Sit in a squatting pose on your feet with your heels pressing into your perineum (the area between your anus and*

scrotum (for men) or clitoris (women), with your palms on your thighs. If this is uncomfortable, you can sit with a pyramidal-shaped cushion between your thighs – so long as it is applying a pleasurable amount of pressure on your genitals.

◆ *Breathe into your root center (the chakra situated in the pelvis just above your heel). Stretch your abdomen upward, lengthening your spine as you inhale.*

◆ *Breathe deeply, and while holding your breath let your head gently drop back, lengthening your throat and allowing your jaw to loosen and relax. Bring in your elbows to straighten up the arms, letting your shoulders rise and roll forward.*

◆ *Contract the anus (men) and vagina and clitoris (women), squeezing the love muscle (PC muscle) for as long as feels comfortable.*

◆ *When you can hold your breath no longer, release your PC muscles and shoulders, and allow your head to gently return to upright, as you slowly exhale.*

◆ *For the next few breaths, feel the build-up of energy created in your root chakra, and allow it to expand throughout your pelvis. In the next few breaths, encourage*

it to spread from your genitals and pelvis up through your body.

◆ *Repeat this breath cycle at least a dozen times.*

Variation

Practice this energy seal during intercourse. In this case, it's better for both partners to be sitting upright, with the woman astride her lover's lap. This is called the Shakti–Shiva pose.

⋅◦⋅

BUILDING YOUR SEXUAL FIRE WITH
THE LOVE MUSCLE PUMP

 Through Tantric exercises, you can uncover your potential for sexual pleasure. You can nurture the erotic connection between you and your partner, using it to create deeper connections on an emotional and spiritual level. Good love-making requires practice. When your love muscles are strengthened, genital sensation and orgasmic pleasure is improved for both men and women, since the physical strength of your orgasms largely depend on the tone of the pelvic muscles. That's why these are called the love muscles. If you have good muscle tone, you can use these love muscle pumps during sexual arousal and intercourse to increase your sensations. They also increase the power of your sexual energy, intensifying your erotic connection as well as the dynamic energy in your body.

This exercise builds on the previous ritual (see page 230), strengthening your love muscle.

Ritual

◆ *Sit in a relaxed pose, with your legs loosely crossed one in front of the other. Let your arms hang easily and relaxed, with your hands resting on your thighs. Focus on your sex (in the area of your perineum for men, g-spot area inside the vagina for women – see page 324 for instructions on locating the g-spot).*

◆ *Inhale as you visualize your energy ascending the energy channel through the core of your being. This channel starts at the base of your spine (the root chakra) and travels up it to the crown of your head. As you breathe in, pull up your love muscle (PC pelvic floor muscles).*

◆ *Hold your breath as the energy ascends your spine to the brow center in the area of your third eye. While holding your breath, release and squeeze the pelvic floor muscles ten times, slowly pumping your love muscle.*

◆ *Then release your breath, exhaling through your nose. For the next few breaths, concentrate on drawing the force from the energized area of your sex up through the core of your being. Let it permeate and nourish your energy-body.*

69

•⋆•

FEELING EACH OTHER AS AN
ENERGY-BODY: THE SPOON

Your body is concentrated energy. Through Tantra, you contact energy by working through your physical body. In seeing your partner as energy rather than physical form, you can relate to him or her on an energy level, and between you create a unified field of energy. This happens when the frequencies of your individual energy bodies attune and resonate in harmony. By exchanging energy in this way, you harmonize your relationship and create more heartfelt love between you.

You can use this breathing meditation to relax together and connect prior to sex, or as part of love-making, or before going to sleep.

Ritual

◆ *Lie on your left side, with your back to your partner's abdomen. It doesn't matter who is on the outside and who on the inside, but you should both be lying on your side. This aligns the chakras.*

◆ *Use synchronized deep breathing. In Tantric rituals, the man follows the pace of the woman's breath. Start by focusing awareness on your own energy centers (chakras). Imagine your two energy–bodies surrounding you, then expand your awareness to concentrate on the loving connection between you. Float together in the love generated by this universal heart.*

◆ *Concentrate on your breath as you inhale and exhale through your nostrils, then become aware of your partner's breath. Harmonize your breathing with your partner's. Breathe in together, hold, then breathe out together. Pause before breathing in again.*

◆ *The person lying behind can imagine that with every exhalation he or she is sending the energy of their breath into the heart center in their partner's subtle body. The person lying in front receives their partner's energy and uses it to expand their own.*

◆ Once your breath is synchronized, start to visualize the breath energizing your chakras at the same time. You can use a color or the symbol for each chakra (see page 75) to help you see the energy field of each center. One partner can say the name of the chakra so that you are both focusing your awareness in the same place.

◆ Starting at your base chakras together at the base of the spine, imagine that your in-breaths are pulling energy into this center. After four or five breaths, move up to the next chakra together. Breathe into this center for a few minutes, then progress through each chakra in turn (see chakra map on page xv).

◆ After you have breathed into the crown chakra, at the top of your hands, lie in each other's arms, imagining the marriage of your energy–bodies creating a warm, loving field of energy. Relax into this warmth and love.

70

• ◦ •

LINGAM MEDITATION

 According to the *Brhadaranyaka Upanishad*, ritual sex is seen as the final offering in fire ritual. In the "five fires sacrifice", faith is offered and the believer receives amrita, the ambrosial nectar. This ambrosia is offered to the god of rain, who in turn is offered to the earth to nourish her and produce food. Food is offered to man, and in man seed is created. This is offered through semen, entailing the creation of new life.

The male role in creation is recognized in Tantra through worshipping the lingam. Both man and woman are needed for the ultimate act of creation, which is why the phallic lingam is usually depicted inside a yoni (vulva) in Tantric carvings. The lingam is represented as solid, potent, erect, proud and shapely.

This solo meditation encourages you to be proud of your own penis. Respect your sexual organ as well as enjoying it. The ritual heightens awareness of the innate power of creation represented by the lingam. It expands your awareness of your penis beyond its capacity to provide sexual pleasure. Through this meditation you can nourish your creativity at a more profound level. Align yourself with your divine nature through embracing the power of your lingam, for yourself and your partner.

Ritual

◆ *Lay down comfortably, and start by slowing and deepening your breath (see breathing meditations, pages 10 and 14).*

◆ *Focus your awareness in the root of your penis, behind your scrotum. Breathe into that place. Feel a sense of expansion. Feel the energy moving around your lingam, and let it tingle with energy.*

◆ *Take this awareness with you as you walk into your own secret garden. There is no-one else in this place but you. Feel your virility, your ability to be omni-fertile. Use your sexual energy to connect with nature. See the plants and flowers as sexual beings: see their sexual parts – the petals and stamens. Visualize the dance of the insects as a sexual dance, as you watch them make love to the flowers. See birds with their mates; a pigeon doing a courtship dance for its mate, a peacock spreading his feathers.*

◆ *As you see the whole of nature in its abundant fertility, let yourself be overwhelmed by the experience. Let this sense of the abundance of nature feed your own sensuality and expand your sense of sexual energy. You are the great god playing with mother earth. See her mountains as breasts, her hillocks as curves. See her caves as her yoni (vulva and vagina), and rivers as her nourishing juices. Feel yourself sporting with the great goddess as you wander through her bounty. See her everywhere, in lakes, clouds, crevices …*

Meditation has really helped me to integrate my sexuality with my whole being. I used to find it difficult to relax enough to focus my mind in the way meditation requires. Because I enjoy sex, the idea of meditating on my penis amused me enough to try it. It felt bombastic at first, but now I genuinely enjoy spending time thinking about how the essence of me is expressed through my penis. When I'm in touch with my sexual nature, that's who I really am.

71

YONI MEDITATION

The moon is a flask of emerald stained with musk, filled with
water and camphor light, which you, for your pleasure,
empty daily, and the creator fills for you again and again.

SAUNDARYALAHARI

The purpose of this meditation is to increase
awareness of your own feminine power, acknowledging the profound ways in which you participate in the
mysteries of creation. Your personal power is fed by
transpersonal energies, and this meditation aligns you to the
feminine as the source of life. It also fosters respect and
pleasure in your own sexual organs, clearing away any
shame or other negative feelings you may have about your
genitals. This ritual helps women get in touch with the

feminine energy of the goddess, and feel the sense of erotic empowerment that this brings.

Ritual

◆ *Make an altar (see page 38), with red and white flowers and light some candles and an oil burner or incense to scent the air.*

◆ *If you are using incense, waft the incense smoke around yourself to purify the environment before making yourself comfortable sitting or lying on the cushions, on a red silk scarf.*

◆ *Lay in a fish posture, if this is comfortable for you: outstretched with your legs crossed, as in lotus posture, with your arms crossed above your head at the wrists.*

◆ *Visualize that you are floating in the water. Let your breath deepen and slow down as you enter a state of meditation.*

◆ *Take your breath right down to your belly. Imagine that your womb is breathing in and out. With each breath allow your womb to relax, releasing your abdomen and letting vital energy flow into your genitals.*

◆ *Focus your attention on your yoni (vulva and vagina).*

246

Allow your vagina to receive the energies of the universe. From this absorption, visualize drops of moisture that appear and accumulate like dew in the lunar light of dawn. Feel the coolness of these dewdrops on your body and on your genitals.

◆ *Imagine that your vulva is the entrance to a well of pleasure. See your womb as a fertile lake, the source of all life. It is a calm pool of water, pale blue and tranquil. Think of your womb as vast, capable of nourishing the whole of creation. Through your sexual energy, you are the source of all creation.*

◆ *Through your yoni, water rains down on creation, feeding and rejuvenating all plant life, all animal life. Your sexual juices replenish the oceans, lakes, and sacred rivers. Your sexual secretions are ambrosia, food of the immortals. They nourish your own psychic centers and those of your lover. Your sexual nature is the source of bliss.*

Variation

You may wish to start the meditation by gazing at the kali yantra for several minutes. Place it in your altar (see page 38).

72

YONI MASSAGE

Once I focused on letting go of my negative feelings something pure and divine occurred inside my vagina. It felt silky and indescribably soft. That softness spread throughout my body. It was an exquisitely delicate state of ecstasy, like an orgasm but much more refined. Now, when I focus on my yoni, I get a sensation of fine energy streaming up through my chakras.

The purpose of the yoni massage is to lovingly explore your partner's vagina and vulva, focusing on touching her in different ways without being distracted by your own sensations. Devote all your attention to discovering what she enjoys.

For the woman, the yoni massage is also an important exercise for deepening trust. It's important to feel you are in charge, and to tell your partner what you enjoy or if there's anything you don't like him doing. Keep the channels of communication open, giving each other feedback during and afterwards.

Ritual

◆ *Connect with your partner with a heart meditation (see page 198). The man honors yoni (see page 200) or anoints her body (see pages 218 and 222).*

◆ *Your partner lies comfortably on her back, on a nest of quilts and pillows. Sit by her side, or between her open legs. Gaze at each other, establishing a loving heart connection. After some minutes, rest your left hand over her heart center while your right hand cups her pubic mound, connecting love and sex.*

◆ *After several minutes, start to massage her whole body gently with almond oil. Use different strokes and pressures. Make sure every touch is gentle.*

◆ *Massage all around the pelvis, including the band of muscles along the top of her pubic area, and along her groin and the tops of her thighs. Firm pressure in these areas helps release tension. Finish by gently stroking the pubic area.*

- *If you (the woman) have any resistance to receiving this massage, focus on resolving it. For example, if you worry that your partner must be bored, or you feel uncomfortable with your genitals exposed, or critical that your partner is not touching you in the right way, communicate your needs, or create an affirmation such as "I enjoy my lover's appreciation of me."*

- *Re-establish eye contact and ask your partner whether she is ready for you to start massaging her yoni. Pour a small quantity of unscented oil or lubricant into your cupped palm, to warm it, and anoint the outer lips of the yoni. Then slowly massage the vulva. Check that she is enjoying the pace and pressure of your touch. Spend some time admiring your lover's genitals, and tell her what you like about them.*

- *Try gently squeezing each of the outer and inner lips between your thumb and forefinger, sliding your fingers up and down the entire length. Gently cup her vulva with your hands, for a few moments.*

- *Gently stroke the clitoris with small circles and gentle squeezes. Encourage your partner just to relax into any erotic sensations. Experiment with dispersing the sexual*

energy that is building by stroking it from the pelvis area up toward the abdomen. Or, you can increase her excitement with blended stimulation – stroking and circling a nipple with your free hand.

◆ *When your partner is ready, slowly slide the middle finger of your right hand inside her vagina. Begin to gently explore the inside of the vagina in every direction, and massage it. The rest of your hand can rest on, or massage, the pubic mound. Vary the depth, speed, and pressure of your fingers. Try small circles, vibrating on any areas that feel numb, and just holding.*

◆ *With your palm facing up, and the middle finger inside the yoni, move the middle finger in a beckoning gesture, exploring the spongy tissue of the g-spot (see page 324). You can move side to side, back and forth, or in circles with your middle finger.*

◆ *Keep breathing and looking into each other's eyes, massaging until she tells you to stop. Very slowly and gently remove your hands. Allow her to just lie still, and enjoy the afterglow, or embrace. If orgasm does occur during the massage it can feel more satisfying and intense than usual, as the exquisite sensations are expanded throughout the body.*

73

MASSAGING YOUR LOVER'S LINGAM

It's important to massage your partner's lingam (penis) with an open heart. In this way you connect your heart and soul with his sexual pleasure. As he experiences pleasure, encourage him to open his heart, at the same time that you open yours.

As a man, celebrate your penis as a source of enormous pleasure. Allow yourself to relax into that pleasure. Accept the experience, however it is, and fall into your sensations. This massage will expand your awareness of arousal and orgasm, and encourage your enjoyment of the different sensations and moods of your lingam during stimulation.

Ritual

TO THE MAN

The goal of lingam massage is not orgasm – although it may happen. Try not to think about whether you will, or will not, achieve an erection or orgasm; just enjoy the massage and relax. Allow yourself to feel your responses, without thinking that you have to respond in any way. It is essential to learn to receive your lover's sensual attention, without feeling you have to perform.

TO THE WOMAN

Focus on massaging your partner's lingam in a sensual, rather than sexual, manner. It is preferable if his lingam (penis) is soft or semi-erect so that you can explore playful ways to touch this sensitive area. Massage his lingam from the base up. Throughout the massage, help your lover disperse sexual feelings from his genitals by stroking the energy up his abdomen and chest toward his heart area. You can then hold your hand over his heart chakra, gazing at him lovingly.

Occasionally, spread the energy across the chest right down to the fingertips, and down his thighs into his legs.

Variation

Experiment with your own penis reflexology (see page 132).

STROKES FOR THE LINGAM

◆ *Tease the lingam – with breath, feathers, tongue, fingernails, hair, breasts.*

◆ *Lightly squeeze, rub, and massage.*

◆ *Roll the lingam between both hands, as if you're slowly making fire.*

◆ *Gently stretch the skin of the lingam from base to head. You can twist the skin slightly.*

◆ *Create a ring with your fingers to delicately hold the scrotum.*

◆ *Form a ring with the thumb and forefinger of one hand at the base of the lingam, and with your other hand gently stretch the skin up around the glans.*

◆ *Hold the base of the penis with one hand and massage the sensitive frenum (on the underside, where the foreskin joins the glans) with the other.*

◆ *Massage the chakra points up and down the penis.*

◆ *Play!*

74

YOGA POSTURES

 Hatha yoga was used by Indian Tantrics to develop suppleness and breath control for purification. *Ha* means "sun" and *tha*, "moon", explaining its purpose as a way of balancing the solar and lunar aspects of the energy–body. Hatha yoga gets the breath moving around the body, and helps you learn to breathe into different parts of your body. It grounds your energy in your hips, and encourages the release of any tension held around the hips and pelvis.

Ritual

◆ *Start with squatting. (This is an important posture for active love-making postures where the woman is on top.)*

◆ *To get into a squat, stand with your feet hip-width apart, and keep your feet parallel (facing forwards) as you bend your knees and sit on your haunches, moving into a squatting position. Your weight should be on your heels, with your buttocks hovering just above the floor. As your hips and ankles relax into the posture, relax the top half of your body, letting your head hang forward and arms drop loosely between your knees. Sit for several minutes at least, breathing into your lower abdomen. With each out-breath, focus on relaxing all the muscles around your hips and pelvis.*

◆ *Move into the corpse posture. This is the posture Shiva (the male) takes when Kali is making love with him in active mode (see page 194), or during her period (see page 304). To get into this posture, lie flat on your back on the floor, with arms relaxed by your side and palms facing upward. To lengthen your back and straighten the spine, start with your knees bent upward and focus on relaxing the small of your back, settling it into the floor. When your back is comfortable, lengthen your neck by drawing your chin down more toward your chest. With your next few breaths, straighten your legs so they lie along the floor, with your feet slightly apart.*

Spend several minutes relaxing.

- *Move back into the posture of release, bringing your knees up again with the soles of your feet resting flat on the floor and the small of your back snuggling into the floor. Place your hands, palms down, over your heart area, and focus on breathing into your heart. Let your arms fully relax, with your elbows resting on the floor. Your fingertips touch each other.*

- *As in the butterfly exercise (see page 260), practice taking your knees to the side as you breathe in, taking the breath all the way down to the base of your abdomen. Exhale, and relax into the posture with a feeling of surrender.*

- *Take another breath in, and as you exhale, press your feet together and downward into the floor in order to bring your knees back to the upright position. If this is at all uncomfortable for your back or hips, support each thigh with cushions.*

- *Once you have familiarized yourself with this "out-in" movement of your legs, switch your attention back to the rise and fall of your abdomen with your breath. Continue for several minutes.*

- *Move to the posture of surrender. This is good for both men and women, enabling you to focus your attention on*

drawing your breath in and out through your genitals. Lay on your back, with your arms out to the side, palms up. Let your knees drop to the floor on either side, placing the soles of both feet together. If you are not very flexible, don't bend your knees quite so much, but leave the soles of your feet together. As you inhale, draw the energy in through your genitals and the base of your spine, imagining it climbing along the spinal cord, and coming to rest in the crown of your head at the end of the inhalation. As you exhale, let the breath drop back down to your genitals.

75

OPEN YOUR PELVIS TO PLEASURE

I haven't met anyone for whom receiving pleasure isn't
a taboo. It's a big step just to let go of the simple taboo
against pleasure.

JOHN HAWKEN, SKYDANCING TANTRA TEACHER

This exercise helps you open to pleasure by increasing your sensitivity to subtle sensations around your
pelvis. It is helpful if either of you have an orgasmic problem.

The technique is an adaptation of a yoga posture called
the butterfly, where you sit with a straight spine and open
out your hips by bending your knees and placing the soles of
your feet together. While sitting in this position you gently
jiggle your hips, to loosen and release any muscle tension
there. If your hips feel stiff, you can just do the butterfly, then

progress as your flexibility improves.

You can use the visualization at the end of the ritual to unblock any psychological resistance to receiving pleasure. If you suffer from a lack of sensitivity in your pelvis, this exercise will help to invigorate this area. (You could precede this with Kundalini shaking [see page 291].)

Ritual

◆ *Make yourself comfortable on your back, lying on a thick quilt. You and your partner can lay side by side. Bend your knees in order to let the small of your back rest on the floor. Lengthen your neck, relaxing your jaw, shoulders, and hands. Make sure that your shoulders are not crunched up, and that your neck is not straining when you raise your pelvis off the floor.*

◆ *Lay there for several minutes, breathing deeply to release stress or strain anywhere in your body. When you feel relaxed, lift your buttocks slightly, taking your weight on your feet and knees in order to gently bounce your pelvis up and down on the floor. Make the movement faster, slower, or more or less vigorous until your pelvis feels alive.*

◆ *Play some dynamic music to stimulate your energy as you*

*awaken it. The music should become softer and more
tranquil after ten minutes.*

◆ *Explore the rhythms of the music you have chosen. Move
and rock your pelvis, allowing it to lift off the floor with
ease.*

◆ *When you feel that your body is charged, stop moving and
concentrate on the vibrations that arise in your pelvis.
Encourage them to spread and to move up your body.
Keep your body relaxed, and allow your knees to gradually
open out. Rather than letting your knees flop right outward, try to hold them open, allowing yourself to feel the
small tremors in your thighs that arise when you hold
them apart. As you hold that position, relax into the sensations until they diminish. Move in tiny movements if you
feel any slight strain or tension.*

This is a way of learning to relax even when your muscles are
tense, rather like building to an orgasm. Try saying "Yes" out
loud each time you open out your legs, to give yourself permission to experience the sensations as they arise. If saying
yes is too embarrassing, try saying, "Ah", releasing your
breath in a relaxed way with each opening of your thighs.

If you do this exercise with your partner present, ask them to sit by your side, gazing into your eyes as you open your legs in time to the music. Allowing your partner to witness this opening up is very intimate. If you feel embarrassed, consider how much it is a privilege for them to see you in this way, and that it brings you into much greater intimacy.

◆ *Let the energy spread from your pelvis, thighs, and genitals up your body. You can use your hand and your breath to sweep or draw the sensations up from your abdomen into your heart. If your partner is present, imagine sending this energy to them through your heart center. Focus on opening your heart, allowing a sense of joy to permeate your being.*

While meditating on your partner's yoni, say "Just as I am entering this yoni, so have I emerged. The Tantric path is as straight as an arrow, but if I follow it without wisdom it will lead me back in countless rebirths. When I enter with knowledge, it becomes the great moon elixir."

CHANDAMAHAROSANA TANTRA

These postures are fun, but you need to be agile to follow them. If you are supple and able to squat for any length of time, try these athletic love-making yoga positions as a variation on anything you have tried before.

Ritual

The Great Moon Elixir Tantra (*Chandamaharosana Tantra*) describes these postures to be followed in sequence. Start the sequence when you are aroused and both ready for penetration. The man squats comfortably on his heels. Clasp your lover round the waist to enter her, as she holds onto your neck or shoulders. She will put her legs around your thighs while you remain squatting (if you are supple) or semi-kneeling, remaining inside her. Then wind your arms around each other like the serpent winding itself around a staff, and start rocking back and forth by each leaning backward in turn. After some time, the woman pulls her knees up against your chest to accentuate the swinging motion. While you hold her around the waist, she rests her feet on your thighs and rubs them while pressing her yoni (genitals) into you.

Next, she slides her buttocks down to the ground and leans back on the bed, pulling you down to hover above her. Caress her breasts in this position, before drawing her back up into a squatting pose, where she explores stretching her legs out to the side, one at a time. This varies the angle of your penetration.

When she wants to, she turns around and leans forward on some cushions. Gently enter her from behind, while massaging her whole body to sensitize her skin and stimulate her energy.

Then return to the upright position and make love more energetically. You can try hooking the back of your lover's knees with your bent elbows.

Next, let her lay down on her back, placing a leg on each of your shoulders. In this position you can explore shallow thrusting, or deep thrusting where you barely withdraw but

stay deep inside, using circular motions and varying your angle and pressure. She can try rocking herself against you with one leg still on your shoulder and the other one resting on your thigh, tilting the angle of her pelvis slightly. Then she can put the soles of both feet together, resting on the middle of your chest, while lying on her back. Both of you, focus on the heart energy stimulated in this posture.

She can finish by blessing you with the soles of her feet, gently touching your mouth, ears, face, and forehead with her soles.

77

THE WAY OF PLEASURE: PLEASURING YOUR PARTNER

 Make sex a priority. Learn to expand your sexual repertoire and deepen your soul connection. In order to experience more pleasure in your life, it is important to set aside time to give and receive pleasure regularly. Try exploring an hour of pleasure every night. What could be more pleasurable than spending time with your lover making love?

Consider making an agreement with your partner not to refuse each other sex and that in principle you will always be responsive to each other's needs. This is a way of avoiding power games in which sex is bartered or withheld. Agree to make love with your partner whenever there is a sexual charge between you, or find ways to connect if for some reason you feel disconnected. Making such a commitment doesn't imply making love in ways you're not happy with. Use it as a way of opening to the erotic charge of your relationship and saying yes to more pleasure.

Ritual

For this exercise, pleasure your partner in the ways that he or she enjoys (see yoni and lingam massages on pages 248–55), while asking for feedback, guidance, and affirmation. A good preparation for this exercise is to observe your partner indulging in self-pleasuring. That way you can use similar techniques to those that they enjoy when they pleasure themselves.

In order to serve your partner, you need to tune into their needs, immersing yourself in what you are doing for, and with, them. If you feel your mind wandering, look at their face or into their eyes if they are open, imparting love through your gaze.

Start by stroking and stimulating their whole body. Rather than going straight for the genitals, touch, kiss, and caress their flesh, enjoying the texture, pressure, and movement of energy. Explore massage, erotic touch, awakening the senses, sensory massage, genital massage, g-spot stimulation, oral sex…

While touching your partner, keep the channels of communication open. Ask for their guidance. Ask what they want. Ask how it feels. Encourage them to describe their inner state. Is there anything else they want from you?

78

•◆•

SELF-PLEASURING

I was in the mood to pleasure myself. I lit some candles and a
stick of incense before crushing some of the petals from my
garland of marigolds into a bowl of water. I anointed my
body with oil, appreciating the soft contours of flesh under
my palm, while looking in the mirror to appraise my body
as if through the eyes of a god. I have the delectable form
of a goddess.

 Self-pleasuring is the key to sexual exploration. As
self-love, it expresses your commitment to exploring
your erotic nature.

This ritual helps you to expand your sexual pleasure, letting go of mechanical or habitual ways of stimulating yourself
in order to discover new and sensations. Once you learn how

to extend your erotic enjoyment, you can share this knowledge with your beloved. If you are not in a relationship currently, or your partner is away, you can explore some of the rituals in this book in conjunction with self-pleasuring.

◆ *Through self-pleasuring you can focus in on your own subtle sensations.*

◆ *Learn how to use your love muscle to improve your orgasmic response (see page 56).*

◆ *Use the love muscle pump to move energy from your pelvis through your energy-body (see pages 60 and 234).*

◆ *Experiment with breathing techniques (see pages 166 and 168).*

◆ *Sense or visualize the movement of energies through the energy centers in your body (see pages 74, 86 and 214).*

◆ *Use self-pleasuring to initiate your lover into your own unique sexual process. Invite them to witness while you self-pleasure your pearl (clitoris) or lingam for half an hour or so. Then let your partner take over, while you tell him or her what feels good and what you would like. Try different strokes and rhythms, without seeking the goal of orgasm.*

Ritual

Sit in front of a mirror, or in front of your partner. As you anoint your skin with massage oil, appreciate your body. Enjoy the shapes your hand defines as it follows the contours of your limbs. Enjoy the textures of your skin as you stroke and rub, massage or caress your body.

Explore your body as if you were your own lover. Treat the experience like a meditation, relaxing into it. Take your time, exploring different touches. Stroke yourself with a feather, your hands, talcum powder, or massage oil. Discover the sensitivity of different areas, paying particular attention to those you habitually neglect. Bring one hand to rest over your pubic mound, and the other between your breasts (at your heart center). Feel a connection between the two centers, your awareness being stimulated by your touch.

TO THE WOMAN

Oil your genitals all over – your inner thighs, vulva, inner lips, and your anus. Explore the delicate skin on the inside of your thighs, perhaps stroking your breasts at the same time. Touch your inner and outer lips, and all the surfaces of your genitals. Play around the clitoris, perhaps using a finger on each side to rub up and down. Circle around the clitoris, or gently rub the hood over the clitoris. Take plenty of time in order to immerse yourself in your own pleasure.

TO THE MAN

Oil your genitals all over – your inner thighs, penis, scrotum, and anus. Explore the delicate skin on the inside of your thighs. Explore all the surfaces of your genitals. Try different strokes and ways of touching yourself. Use your hand to hold your lingam (penis) with thumb facing up or down. Use one hand or two. Use your hand to make a ring. Roll your penis between your hands, or use rhythmic stroking movements up and down its length. Cradle your scrotum, and rub or gently squeeze. Rub the fleshy mound behind your scrotum, which is the external prostate spot. As you get aroused, you may like to explore the perineum (the area between the scrotum and anus) and the anus, as this area becomes more pleasurable as the root of the penis gets more engorged with blood.

79

THE SUBTLE ENERGIES IN
LOVE-MAKING

I was inside him and he was inside me. Words shaped the
experience, reshaping my body, dissolving its boundaries.
Who was man, who was woman, no longer mattered, just
the smooth, taut skin.

Tantric rituals are about uniting the polarities
between you and your lover, masculine and feminine, sun and moon, white and red. This exercise involves
exploring the solar (focused) and lunar (devotional) polarities
in your relationship. You may already notice these poles, but
you will become more aware through consciously exploring
them. Your eventual aim is to transcend polarities so there is
no longer giver and receiver, doer or done-to, lover or loved

one, but only love. See also the sun–moon game (page 32). This ritual deepens the love between you by invoking the strong energy connections created by the power of your sexual attraction. Tantra sees this magnetic attraction as a powerful force for self-development and spiritual growth.

With the lingam (penis) inside the yoni (vagina) in a relaxed way, the positive and negative electrical poles of the sexual centers are balanced. Tantrics believe that the lingam delivers a healing energy just by being inside the yoni when the contact between your genitals is gentle and healing, rather than vigorous and exciting. Being inside the yoni in this quiet, receptive way is healing for both of you.

Ritual

Start with heart-to-heart breathing (see pages 14 and 26) or a radiant energy meditation (page 174). This helps you celebrate your love-making with joy and delight, connecting and opening your heart to each other to share your mutual pleasure and increase your receptivity to sexual energy. Begin this ritual when you feel aroused by gentle, loving sexual contact and wish to have intercourse.

TO THE MAN

Let the excitement in your lingam (penis) spread outward, enveloping your whole body as you become completely identified with your lingam. Let your pleasure take the form of light, so that your penis/body becomes a beacon radiating light. Imagine that your penis is radiant with light as you slowly penetrate your lover. Let waves of light emanate

from your lingam, illuminating the body of your lover from inside.

TO THE WOMAN

As you breathe, imagine that your whole body is aroused, allowing the excitement to spread from your genitals until your entire body becomes a warm, juicy fruit. As your lover enters you, embrace his phallus with your whole being. Imagine that the lingam (penis) inside your yoni (vagina) is a source of light that permeates your pelvis and whole body. Send out waves of love with each out-breath.

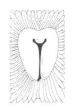

80

. ◦ ◦ .

SUCKING THE JUICES OF LOVE

When he has embraced his partner and inserted his scepter
into her lotus, he should drink heavily from her lips, which
are sprinkled with milk. As the full richness of delight is
enjoyed, her thighs begin to quiver and her first fulfillment
is reached. This is the way of becoming one with the
imperishable, by absorbing each other selflessly.

KALACHAKRA TANTRA

 New Age teacher Barry Long suggests that the
divine alchemy of sex only takes place when a man
expresses enough love in his love-making to connect with
the soul of his lover. This is the key to extracting the divine
energies that Tantras regard as the essence of woman. This
deep love is a sign of an evolved masculinity. Only by

unreservedly opening to love can a man assimilate the female energies released during love-making.

The most sophisticated Tantric sexual practice involves making love after ejaculating in such a way as to mix the semen together with female ejaculate. Then the man uses his penis like a straw to suck the woman's sexual fluids inside his body, and the woman focuses on absorbing this mixture through her vaginal walls. This is known as the posture (mudra) of immortality, because the love juices nourish our vitality.

Ritual

In this exercise, the man focuses on absorbing the lunar qualities of a woman's juices through his phallus, while she concentrates on absorbing the masculine, solar qualities of his secretions through her vaginal walls. You can do this before ejaculation if you need to avoid conception.

Start with an open heart meditation (see page 198). Let your love flow freely as you meditate, and celebrate your desire for each other. Opening your heart during lovemaking helps you to receive sexual energy through your genitals. Concentrate on expressing your love through your own genitals during sex, and feel the love in your partner's genitals as you make love.

TO THE WOMAN

Embrace your lover's phallus with your whole being. Send out waves of love with each out-breath. When he is inside you, receive the solar, masculine qualities of the lingam (penis), and imagine absorbing its heat and passion through your vaginal walls. Let these qualities nourish your energy-body.

TO THE MAN

Let the excitement in your lingam (penis) spread outward, until your body becomes an enormous lingam. Imagine that your penis is radiant with love as you enter her yoni (vagina). Let waves of love pour into her body as you make love. Feel the watery, cooling qualities of her yoni, absorbing the heat of your lingam. Let these qualities harmonize your subtle internal metabolism, nourishing and softening you. Visualize absorbing your lover's lunar energies through your penis.

AFTER MAKING LOVE

After making love, leave your lingam inside her yoni so that the juices can mingle and be absorbed. Women can use the love-muscle squeeze (see page 56) to milk their partner of his juices. Men can squeeze their love muscle and imagine sucking up the love juices, as if their penis were a straw. Suck her tongue at the same time, absorbing the unique essence of her saliva and mixing it with your own.

·◆·

81

DRINKING AT THE SACRED SOURCE: CUNNILINGUS

With his head resting between her thighs, the adept drinks
deeply from the source of life. Above, the goddess causes his
power to grow and transform into the wisdom fields inside
her mind, while below, he enters each wave of wisdom
according to his ability. Each meditates on the
transcendental experience of non-duality, until the
confluence of rivers swells and bursts its banks.

CHANDAMAHAROSANA TANTRA

 The tongue is considered an important focus for channeling subtle energies. When both lovers tongue each
other's genitals, an energy circuit (mudra) is created between
your two bodies, uniting them as one. Mixing love juices and

saliva is important for sexual alchemy. As you drink from your lover's genitals, meditate on drinking from the fountain of life. The yoni (female genitalia) is the birthplace of the goddess, and when you please her she will grant you many favors.

Ritual

Create a sacred space (see page 38) with soft lighting, incense, and some evocative, heartful music. Begin with a namaste (see page 2).

TO THE WOMAN

◆ *Invite your partner to sit in your temple in front of you. Start to dance, enjoying your own gestures and movements and absorb yourself in the shapes you're making. Celebrate life and all its delights.*

◆ *Show off to your lover, inviting him to join you in your appreciation of your own body. Express yourself to him through movements and gestures. Honor him, love him, tantalize him. Remove layers of clothing as you dance.*

◆ *Continue to dance, showing off your beautiful form. Show the different aspects of your breasts, your thighs, your yoni. Show him your sex.*

◆ *Caress yourself if you like, and your yoni, until he is sitting before you with his tongue literally hanging out. Tantalize him by waving your yoni in front of his face, teasing him with its proximity. You can sit on the edge of the bed with your legs apart as he kneels on the floor. He can worship you with his tongue, tasting your yoni juice and absorbing its potent essence.*

TO THE MAN

◆ *Concentrate on the yoni's particular flavor and texture, allowing yourself to fully experience it. Approach your lover with reverence, honoring her genitals (see page 190) as you taste them.*

◆ *Play with her vulva, licking her from the vagina to the clitoris in long, loving strokes. Breathe out your cool breath on her wet lips, and inhale her unique scent. Circle her pearl (clitoris) with your firm tongue, before softly biting or sucking it to encourage her to release her love juices.*

◆ *Stay with what she enjoys, maintaining a steady pace and rhythm as her excitement mounts. She will appreciate you continuing for as long as possible – keep up the stimulation with your fingers when your tongue needs a rest. Taste her*

love juices, appreciating her abundance. Imagine her sexual fluids as the nectar of bliss, created during the divine sexual congress of the goddess Shakti and her consort, Shiva.

THE SACRED ESSENCES OF THE BODY

In Tantra, sex is an intermingling of body fluids, as well as an energetic meeting. Body fluids are considered sacred, because they are the essence of you and your Beloved. In the Tantra tradition, techniques for the mutual absorption of fluids include the exchange of saliva through kissing, drinking from a woman's breast, and the exchange of genital secretions during oral sex. Yoni essence is considered a sacred fluid.

82

TASTING LINGAM: FELLATIO

Honor your lover as Lord Shiva, his lingam
as the male principle.

Behold the Shiva lingam, beautiful as molten gold, firm as
the Himalayan mountain, tender as a folded leaf, life-giving
like the solar orb; behold the charm of his sparkling jewels.

LINGA PURANA

 The art of oral sex is the art of arousing the seed of
Shiva by dancing around his phallus like a snake goddess coiled around his lingam. During oral sex, honor the
lingam as if it encompasses the male principle, a symbol of
Lord Shiva, the ultimate lord and lover. This ritual encourages
you to treat your partner's penis with a reverence he will def-

initely enjoy. You can drink the elixir of life directly from its source (page 294).

Ritual

◆ *Set up a sacred space (see page 38) in front of an open fire, or with candles and incense. Place fresh flowers in bowls of water to represent fire. Prepare food, drink, and choose some atmospheric music.*

◆ *Cleanse your body by taking a shower or a bath together. Decorate the bathroom with lit candles and bowls of roses, scattering rose petals in the bath water. (Bathing is always better before rather than after sex, when you should leave your partner's love juices on your skin.)*

TO THE MAN

◆ *Get your lover in the mood by performing a slow and sensuous striptease, revealing your body bit by bit. Then put on a favorite piece of music and dance for her, moving your body freely and allowing your genitals to join the dance. Let your lover appreciate your body in all its supple inventiveness. Tantalize her and arouse her admiration for your member.*

◆ *Invite her to caress your body, and your lingam.*

◆ *Start by holding your lover's penis and scrotum cupped gently in your hands. Then start to slowly caress his genitals.*

◆ *Roll the lingam between your hands. Press firmly. Stroke. Tickle.*

◆ *Hold the lingam in your hand, caressing your lips with it.*

◆ *Hold the head of his penis with your fingers while mouthing the sides of the stalk. Lick the underside of his penis, from the seam in his scrotum, to the deliciously sensitive "v" shape where the foreskin meets the head of the penis.*

◆ *Kiss your lover's lingam as if it were his lips. Play your tongue over all its surfaces. Discover the areas your part-ner finds particularly sensitive. Press with your mouth and tongue, and suck and lick the tip as if it were an ice-cream cone. Tantalize your partner with swallowing his penis as far as feels comfortable.*

◆ *Taste his pre-ejaculate as it oozes from the urethra. If he ejaculates, taste his semen, absorbing its essence into*

your being. Visualize it as nourishing your energy, passion, and vitality.

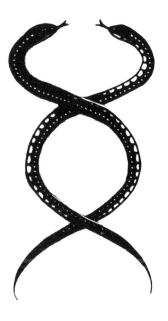

83

·•◆•·

ROBE YOUR LOVER

 In Indian Tantric rituals, men are usually made up to resemble Shiva, an ascetic yoga master, who carries a three-pronged trident symbolizing his consciousness which penetrates all creation. White wood ash is smeared all over their bodies, and sets of three horizontal lines are marked in black bands on the forehead, chest, upper arms, and shins. Women are made up with henna, coloring red the navel, the palms of the hands, and the soles of the feet. The patterns can be beautifully ornate. The third eye, or brow, chakra is marked with a red vertical line above the root of the nose. This chakra should be open during sacred sex, and marking it helps concentrate the energy there.

In this ritual, you prepare for sacred sex by robing your lover as befits a god or goddess. This exercise is about paying positive attention to your partner's appearance, appreciating the variety of ways they look lovely, and experimenting with different styles of accenting their unique beauty. Apply your

sense of aesthetics to the colors and shapes of their under-
wear, clothing, make-up and jewelry. Put their hair up or style
it in different ways. Plait colored threads or beads into their
tresses. Adorn their hair with flowers or headscarves. Enjoy
the process of clothing them, handling them with loving care
and reverence. Be playful and adventurous, trying different
textures and colors and unusual or exotic combinations. Try
on different jewelry, in different places. By paying such close
attention to their form you make them feel good about their
body and appearance. We could all do with more appreciation and adoration.

Ritual

◆ *Wash your lover with rose water, then massage him or her
gently to relax their body, then more energetically to stimulate it. While you anoint his or her body with perfume or
a few drops of essential oil, concentrate on reciting their
name as a mantra, or hum if you prefer.*

◆ *Choose clothes that show off your lover's form, yet are
comfortable and loose enough for them to move without
restraint. Clothe your beloved in soft fabrics, such as silk
or fine cotton. You might use a kimono, shawls, sarongs, or*

*lingerie. Take time over dressing your lover, commenting
on and appreciating their changing appearance.*

◆ *Honor your beloved, placing a garland around his or her
  neck. Apply body make-up (see henna recipe, page 45),
  and adorn him or her with flowers or jewels as befits a god
  or goddess.*

I envied women the chance to dress up, since men's clothes
are so boring. When my partner told me she wanted to dress
me in silks, I bought a wine-colored shirt and dark-blue
boxers for the occasion.

After a bath together, she laid the clothes out for me in our
bedroom. She dried me and then massaged my body with
talcum powder. I probably haven't been ministered to in this
way since I was a baby. To my surprise, she darkened my
lips with crushed berries and smudged kohl round my eyelids.
When I looked in the mirror, I saw myself as a dashing young
man again. Then her lips covered mine, tasting the blue berries.

84

SACRED SEX: MIXING THE RED
AND THE WHITE

 Tantrics believe that the red and the white elements, which make up the metabolism of female and male bodies, need to be mixed. Red is the color associated with Shakti (female) energy, while white is associated with Shiva (male) consciousness. Red is the color of dynamism, passion, sexual energy, and creativity. White is the color of meditation, yoga, transformation, and transcendence. During lovemaking the red and white energies mingle, rather than merge. Each color remains distinct and powerful in its own right, but open to the enrichment that comes through energy interaction and exchange.

During sex, an alchemical process occurs in which the red primal material of sexuality is processed by the rest of the energy-body and transformed into its spiritual essence. This happens by mixing the red and the white elements that make up the metabolism of female and male bodies. This divine alchemy only takes place when couples unite in love.

Ritual

◆ *Stimulate your energy by showering in cold water, doing yoga postures (page 206) or dancing (page 256), then move into the stillness of meditation for several minutes. Open your hearts to one another.*

◆ *Light a candle on your altar. The woman traditionally sits to the right of her partner. Meditate on the solar–lunar breath together to harmonize your energy–body in the body (see page 166) or do a sun–moon meditation (see page 172).*

TO THE MAN

◆ *Look at your lover with adoration, seeing her as the goddess, Shakti. You represent the god, Shiva. In your sacred space, sit in contemplation of the candle flame or fire to build the solar energy in your body. Return your gaze to her body and trace the lunar energy channels in her body (see page 126).*

TO THE WOMAN

◆ *While your partner is looking at you, visualize yourself as a living goddess, full of love, the crucible in which to transform the passion generated between you. Stimulate your erotic energy by deep breathing and gently rocking your pelvis back and forth. Let dynamic energy fill your being with a heightened charge.*

◆ *Move to the left of your partner, signifying that you are taking an active role as initiator. Perform self-worship by lighting some sticks of incense and circulating them in a clockwise direction around both of you. This cleanses the atmosphere of negative energies and protects you both.*

◆ *Arouse him by moving your hands and lips over his body while holding the image of him as Lord Shiva in your*

mind's eye. Honor his lingam and anoint it with oil, or something that tastes pleasant, such as yoghurt. Take his lingam in your mouth (see page 286), before inviting him to taste your yoni.

◆ Oral sex incorporates and balances sexual fluids and subtle energies between you. When you feel aroused by his tongue, mouth, and hands, invite his lingam inside you, with you either laying down or seated.

TOGETHER

◆ Make love in a slow, loving way, exploring the subtle sensations created by intercourse. Alternate periods of stillness with gentle movement, and the occasional dynamic stirring of his lingam inside your yoni.

◆ Visualize the sexual energy rising up through your united energy-body as one. Circulate this vital energy throughout your whole being, using breathing and visualization. Focus on absorbing it back into your body. The man focuses on absorbing your yoni essence while you absorb his lingam essence. If conception is not a problem, leave the lingam inside the yoni after ejaculation to maximize absorption.

.•◆•.

85

BLESSING YOUR PARTNER WITH YOUR SEXUAL CLIMAX

 The famous mantra Om is considered to be the sound of the universe humming. Yoga masters say that it is only when we have cleared our subtle body enough, and are able to enter states of deep meditation, that we can hear this spontaneous vibration of the universe, which is always resonating with energy. In this exercise, you intone the mantra to align yourselves with universal energy and then share this blessing with your partner at the moment of climax. Blessing means transferring energy to your partner.

Your sexual climax fills you with transpersonal power. This sense of empowerment comes from sexual charge and release, during which you create an energy-body that is the sum of your individual erotic energies. In Tantra, this ritual blessing through orgasm is known as expanded sex, which expresses the potency you experience as energy is transferred between you.

It is important for both of you to have an experience of expanded sex. If you don't reach a climax at the same time, use this ritual to include your partner in your rapture. In your rapture you become more than yourself, offering a gateway to your partner through which they can access their transpersonal nature. Your expanded awareness is a gift to your beloved.

You can try this exercise if you are used to meditating, or after you have tried several of the other meditation practices in this book (such as pages 86, 106, and 316).

Ritual

At the point of orgasm, draw your sexual excitement up the energy channels through the middle of your body, from your genitals to your forehead. At the moment of ejaculation, intone the mantra Om in three parts, as A-u-m and touch your partner's head in empowerment, while imagining this movement of energy. (See page 80 for intoning the mantra Aum).

86

ALTERNATING BETWEEN THE
TWO POLES

 As an experiential path to knowledge, ritual sexual practices balance the gender polarity in women and men, by unifying female and male energies in the body and aligning them with the cosmos.

Parts of the body are mapped as having a positive electrical charge, and other parts negative. For instance, in men, the heart center (located in the middle of the chest) is considered a negative charge and is related to the penis which has a positive charge. It's important to connect these two poles through massage or meditation. Areas with a positive and negative energy charge attract each other, and when you stimulate both together you can produce high states of arousal. The area at the base of the penis going toward the prostate gland (negative) attracts the head of the penis is considered (positive).

Breasts are considered positive, like the pearl (clitoris) and head of the lingam. Stimulating one of these areas will also arouse the others. Balance this stimulation by blending it with a complementary pole, such as the vagina.

The g- (goddess) spot (the pleasure zone inside the vagina) and the clitoris are complementary sexual poles, one inside and one outside the vagina. Both should be stimulated during extended sexual pleasuring, preferably at the same time. These complementary areas feel great when stimulated together (see page 248).

Ritual

◆ *Start with a namaste (see page 2). Gaze at each other, and open your heart to your lover. Then invite your lover to lie down while you sit at his or her side. When the man is giving to his partner, he can sit to her right.*

◆ *Lay one hand palm down over your lover's chest, between the breasts, and one over their genitals. Visualize a strong current of energy connecting and balancing these two chakras (energy centers).*

◆ *Begin to massage your partner's belly, working down to their genitals, before brushing along the skin from their pubic area up toward the chest. When you have done this, hold your hand over the heart center once again.*

◆ *Then lightly massage his chest or her breasts. Stimulate one nipple with your tongue, the other with your hand. Use your fingertips, tongue, teeth, or some feathers. Begin to stimulate your partner's genitals in the same way. Alternate between one and the other, noticing the different qualities of each area. Then stimulate both breasts and genitals together, while the person receiving focuses on the energy connections between them.*

◆ *When your partner becomes very aroused, shift your attention to the two poles within their genital region. For men, alternate between stimulating the base and the head of the penis (the base is the bulbous area behind the scrotum, between the scrotum and anus). Explore the different qualities of sensation. Massage the perineum quite deeply, or if he prefers this area to be stimulated from inside his anus, do so carefully. Massage this area at the same time as you stimulate the head of the penis. He can visualize a sun in the penis and a moon in the prostate while receiving this blended stimulation.*

◆ *When massaging your woman, suck her nipples while you gently stroke and finger her vagina. Spend some time arousing your partner through caressing and licking her*

pearl (clitoris). If she is wet enough, use a finger to rub the upper inside surface of her vagina. Alternate between the pearl and g-spot inside the vagina (see page 336).

◆ *After some time, rub or circle the clitoris while one or two fingers are crooked upward inside to rub her g-spot rhythmically. You can place a thumb on her clitoris while using your fingers to stroke the g-spot. While you are doing this, she imagines the clitoris as a sun, and the vagina as a moon.*

◆ *The receiver can self-pleasure their pearl or lingam while the giver focuses on the g-spot (see page 324), or perineum (page 328). Focus on swinging energy between these two poles, when you are stimulating them alternately. When you are stimulating both, focus on balancing and harmonizing the sensations of each area.*

◆ *If you want to have intercourse, focus on the energy exchange between the positive pole of the head of the penis and the negative pole of the g-spot. Finish with a bonding cuddle.*

SEX DURING MENSES:
CONSORTING WITH KALI

The Tantric adept should view a menstruating woman with
awe and reverence. She is the living embodiment of Kali, the
power of transcendence; her menstrual blood is the flowery
essence of all womanhood, the very blood of life. Possessed
of supernormal qualities, it is a potent rejuvenating and
transforming force, purifying all poisons through its
alchemical fire. By performing sexual rites with a
menstruating woman, the adept advances more
quickly along the path of Liberation.

KAULA TANTRA

 In his book *Tantric Quest*, Daniel Odier writes that in
Tantrism there is one fundamental color: "Red is the

color of the living heart, the color of blood, the color of fire, the color of roses and of the tongue, the color of the open vulva, the color of the erect penis, the color of the sun that warms the hermit, the color of the circle of fire that must be crossed to attain consciousness."

Because of the connection between the moon and menstruation, the phases of a woman's life-cycle are correlated to the monthly phases of the moon. In some Tantric traditions women are viewed as virginal after menstruation, as a young wife for the first week, an experienced wife the second, and a wise woman as menstruation approaches. During menstruation she is seen as existing between two worlds, between the cycle of death and rebirth, a liminal period that is recognized as a potent time for spiritual transformation. The goddess, Kali presides over the dark moon, regulating the forces of disintegration and transformation.

Menstrual blood is charged with the energy of the root, or base, chakra (see page xiv) which makes it extremely potent. Many Tantric rituals involve sex during menstruation. At one of Kali's temples in Assam, India, the naturally reddish-colored water is worshipped as her menstrual blood.

Tantrics see a menstruating woman as an initiator. During

menstruation, your lover embodies the goddess Kali, who presides over the phenomenal cycles of life, death, and rebirth. As such, she is in contact with other worlds, and sexual intercourse during this time can help her lover to access the other world.

Menstruation is considered a potent time for love-making, when a woman takes an active role. During intercourse she sits on top of her partner, riding him like the goddess Kali riding her consort Shiva.

Ritual

◆ *Start with a meditation in order to get in touch with the positive qualities that you associate with menstruation. Focus on how you feel when bleeding. Do you feel earthy, rooted, powerful, vulnerable, cleansed, fluid, sexy, maternal?*

◆ *Ask your partner to honor your body, bending down to touch your ankles, thighs, hips, wrists, and the nape of your neck, before stroking your body all over. He can use slow, energizing strokes, starting at the navel, working up the torso, then down the arms and the legs (see page 152).*

◆ *Take charge of this love-making session, telling your partner what you want.*

◆ *When you are ready for intercourse, sit astride your partner while he lies back in a position of surrender. Hold his chest as you lean over him and take his lingam inside you. Visualize yourself as red, astride your white lover. During intercourse, the man visualizes himself as white, absorbing the energetic qualities associated with redness through his genital contact with your menstrual blood.*

◆ *Take up the camel pose, sitting astride your partner and facing his face, but leaning back and grasping his ankles. This opens out your pelvis, creating a conduit for the transmission of menstrual energy. It also helps his lingam reach your g- (goddess) spot, making intercourse more arousing.*

◆ *Sitting with his penis inside you, churn the sacred blood around, making an offering of your menstrual blood. He imagines that he is absorbing the rejuvenating and life-affirming energies of your blood through his lingam (see page 276).*

88

·•◦•·

HEART BREATH

All I could hear was his breath, my breath, our breath – one breath. As my breath slowed, his followed, keeping pace with my rhythms. It was so gently intimate that it felt like he was witnessing my being. There was no need to do anything else. Just look; just breathe. It was more intimate than lying naked together. I trusted him, and I would follow him on our journey.

 This exercise uses the Tantric technique of imagining your breath climbing through the energy centers in your body, called the chakras. The most important chakras to awaken are the sexual center, the heart, and the brow center (see page 44, and chakra map on page xv).

Opening your heart chakra nourishes loving emotions. This exercise builds your sexual energy by connecting it with love, enriching your relationship. It links sex with heart and then with spirit, as you open your body to the powerful energy fueled by your erotic drive. You power your sexual center in this ritual by breathing in and out of your genitals, then drawing that energy into your heart to activate your love. Finally, you offer your love to your partner.

Ritual

- *Start with a namaste (see page 2).*
- *Stand facing each other, and gaze into each other's eyes.*
- *Inhale together, while you imagine the breath entering through your genitals. Visualize your breathing coming in through your yoni (vagina – or your perineum, the area between the anus and genitals, if you are a man) and then draw it up to the area of your heart. Place one hand over your genitals and the other over your heart, to help you focus on where the breath is going. As you breathe in, draw up your breath from your genitals through the center of your body, coming to rest in the area of your heart by the end of each inhalation.*
- *Pause at the end of the in-breath, focusing on your heart area. Simultaneously release your breath and allow it to*

drop down through the center of your body (in front of your spine), down to the tailbone and out through the base of your spine and genitals.

◆ *Once you both feel comfortable drawing up the heart energy, move your right hand to your partner's chest, laying it over the area of their heart center. With your next out-breath, visualize the energy streaming from your heart into their heart. With your in-breath, inhale the heart energy that is streaming from your partner, and send it back down to your genitals.*

◆ *As you continue breathing in this way for several minutes, focus on letting sexual energy build in your pelvis. With each inhalation, draw this erotic energy up to your heart with each breath. Remain in eye contact with your partner, sharing your joint desire to unite your sexuality and spirituality.*

◆ *Use your right hand to mimic the energy rising from your sex into your heart. As you pause at the end of the in-breath, complete the gesture by moving your hand as if you were offering a beautiful flower, such as a lotus, to your partner. Do this just in front of your heart area, as it is here that your individual energies meet.*

◆ *As your breath falls again, your hand can follow its pathway down the front of your body and back to your sex. This can be helpful to you both in co-ordinating your breathing, as you can see the path of the breath by watching the movements and rhythm of the hand rising and falling. Focus on opening your heart as you connect deeply with your partner.*

Variation

You can extend this exercise by taking the breath up to the higher chakras. Using your hand to gesture will help your partner know when you are moving up from the heart chakra. The woman will signal this changeover with her hand following the breath as it drops down into her sex, and then rises up into the third eye chakra (on your forehead, between your eyes).

After several minutes, bring the energy up to the crown center, at the top of your head.

89

·•·

HEART WAVE

We were making love, reveling in a mood of joy and delight.
Usually when I make love my energy shoots straight up from
my base chakra to my heart, and if my partner is blocked and
can't give, it doesn't work for me. But on this occasion my
partner's heart was open, and we were sharing the joyfulness
of our mutual pleasure. Because of his open heart I could
receive his sexual energy through my yoni, and I felt my
chakras open up one by one. We felt deeply connected. We
were relaxing and looking into each other when my body
clicked naturally into this experience that I'd struggled to
learn. My ecstatic response wasn't about techniques or
breathing in the end, because our bodies were doing that
naturally; it was about being open. I could feel the quality of
my lover's delight, and the clarity of the energy coming
through his penis – without any holding back at all.

In the heart-wave ritual you create an energy connection between you and your beloved, in which you transfer loving, sexual energy to each other at the level of your genitals. Your breath becomes a vehicle for the heart energy to be circulated and exchanged between the two of you by means of your sexual connection.

You start by connecting your heart, then focus on igniting your sexual passion. You and your partner then take turns to send your loving energy downward to each other, warming it with the heat of your passion.

Ritual

◆ *Start with a namaste, bowing to your partner (see page 2).*

◆ *Stand facing each other, and gaze into each other's eyes. Let the love build up in your heart as you gaze at your beloved. Feel how much you love and desire your mate.*

◆ *Fall into slow, deep breathing together. Focus on drawing your breath up through your genitals, into your heart area. With each inhalation, draw the breath upward through the center of your body, coming to rest in the area of your heart by the end of each inhalation.*

◆ *Once you have settled into the same relaxed pace of breathing, fall into an alternate pattern of breathing; as the woman breathes out, her partner breathes in, inhaling her precious breath. You may wish to use hand gestures to demonstrate where your breath is traveling, tracing the passage of air as you imagine drawing it from your genitals up the front of your body to your heart, and then letting your hand drop as the breath goes down again.*

◆ *The woman holds her breath in the area of her heart chakra while her partner breathes out. As he begins to inhale, she releases her breath, visualizing her energy dropping back down to her genitals. She imagines her breath streaming out of her genitals toward those of her partner and shows him with her hand. He breathes in through his genitals and takes her breath up to his heart, incorporating her sexual energy.*

◆ *This energy swings between you in a crescent shape, connecting sex and heart. The points of the crescent represent the points at which you are receiving and giving energy through your breath, exchanging and sharing with your partner.*

Variation

When you have learned how to use the breath to circulate energy between you, try the heart wave during love-making (see page 352, circular breathing during love-making).

Sitting on his lap, we shifted our concentration from our pelvic area to our third eye chakra, then back to the heart area, swinging it back and forth between us. Exhilarating streams of life energy coursed through us. Called "opening the inner flute", this process of moving energy around the energy centers surprised us with its intensity.

90

MEDITATE ON YOUR BREATH
DURING LOVE-MAKING

I kissed her forehead, throat, and nipples, and anointed her chakras with my lips rather than oils. I kissed her chakras all the way down her body, then she did the same to me. We were really turned on, and she sat on my lap with my penis inside her. We stayed quite still, and our breathing naturally harmonized. I imagined a U-shaped tube linking us, with energy sloshing from one side to the other as we breathed in turns. As I breathed in she pulled her hands up my spine, which really helped me to focus.

She was getting very excited, even though we weren't moving much. I felt the energy move up through the tube above my head, almost poised there. It was as if we were two halves of the same vessel. We felt as if a magical fluid was sloshing back and forth. She reached an orgasm plateau, and I felt very excited but knew I wouldn't actually come. That went on for a long time as we sat quite still. I didn't move my pelvis to try and facilitate her orgasm. Instead we sat for some time holding hands, as we'd done at the beginning.

Meditating on your breath and circulating it during love-making creates a single energy-body out of your two physical bodies, and an intense erotic charge. This will give you an experience of sacred sex, in which your sexuality is transformed by focusing on creating a powerful energy connection.

In this ritual, you explore different methods of encouraging the energy to circulate between you and your partner. It can flow in different directions: the active breath (directed out through your genitals and in through your heart) is associated with giving, and the receptive breath with receiving (directed in through your genitals and out through your heart). This technique is to explore active and receptive breaths by breathing in or out through your genitals and heart creating a loving circle of erotic energy between you. In swapping roles during this exercise, you can explore the polarities of giving and receiving with your breath. This will help you balance these qualities in your relationship.

Ritual

◆ *Start by familiarizing yourself with the direction of the breath. Shiva (the man) commence with the active breath, and Shakti the receptive.*

◆ *Once you're both feeling sexually aroused by the breathing and circulating of energy, connect your genitals by moving into the Shiva–Shakti position: make yourselves comfortable with cushions to support your buttocks and thighs, and have the man sit cross-legged with the woman astride him, her legs wrapped around his waist. In Tantra, this transition occurs at the woman's instigation. If she would like her partner to enter her, she invites his lingam inside her yoni, or takes his lingam inside her as she sits on his lap.*

◆ *Shakti (woman): draw your breath in through your vagina from his penis, letting it pass through your heart before directing this loving energy out, through your heart, toward your partner.*

◆ *Shiva (man): as your partner breathes out, you are inhaling her out-breath. As you inhale, imagine pulling her loving heart energy into your heart, as you breathe in, drawing it down into your genitals. As you exhale, send out your erotic love to your partner through the base of your penis.*

◆ *The woman then breathes in, breathing the erotic energy she receives from your genitals into her own, and draws it up to her heart once again.*

◆ *Both maintain eye contact. Explore different rates of breathing; faster, slower, more intense. The active person determines the rate of your breathing, but it's important to harmonize your rhythm with your partner's.*

Experiment with reversing the direction of this cycle of breathing, so that the woman sends her erotic energy out to her partner through her genitals, and receives this transformed energy back through her heart, in the form of loving energy.

91

BREATHING WITH PELVIC ROCKING

He pulled me toward him, nestling me on his lap. We sat entwined on the beach, my red cape pulled around our bodies, making private what was not public. Eyes closed, he tuned into my breathing. I slowed down my out-breath; he slowed the in-breath. Synchronized, I pushed our breath faster and slower, faster and slower. As I felt warmth rising from my pelvis I squeezed my yoni in a quick gasp, pulling up my sexual energy.

With the full moon our witness, I was riding his sex, feeling the fire rising from his pelvis through me and into our upright bodies. Slowly, slowly, he circled his pelvis, encouraging the slow fire to snake up my navel. He held the back of my neck, his tongue probing my mouth with intent.

According to Margo Anand, author of *The Art of Sexual Ecstasy*, there are three main keys to improve your sexual aliveness: movement, breath, and vocalization. This ritual combines all three to enhance your sexual responsiveness. Its aim is to generate sexual arousal through rhythmic movements.

Ritual

◆ *Sit facing each other, at first in the half-lotus position (see page xvi). You can dovetail your positions by both resting your right knee on your partner's left one.*

◆ *Breathe slowly and gently together, harmonizing your breathing. It's good practice to follow the woman's pace, unless her breathing is rapid and shallow, in which case you can calm her by slowing down your own breath. Once your joint breath is established, close your eyes and focus on the movement of breath through the energy channels in your own body.*

◆ *Starting together, as you inhale imagine pulling the breath in through the area of your root chakra. As you release your breath, let it back out through the area around your perineum (between the anus and the genitals). Breathe* for several minutes, imagining the breath entering your genitals via the base of the spine, and receding with every exhalation.

- ◆ Once you have established this pattern, continue breathing in this way and introduce a gentle forward-tilt of the pelvis (with genitals facing downward) as you breathe in, then tilt backward (with genitals facing toward each other), as you breathe in.

- ◆ The woman moves on to the next chakra when ready: draw your breath in through your yoni (vagina) and up to the second chakra in your navel, as you rock your pelvis and hips gently backward (with your yoni forward). Your partner can join you with his next in-breath.

- ◆ Keep rocking the pelvis, both of you bringing your energy up to the second chakra. With every inhalation bring your hips forward, and with every exhalation, tilt your hips backward.

- ◆ Continue this exercise, drawing up your breath from your genitals to each chakra in turn while you gently rock the pelvis and squeeze your love muscle (see page 56) with each breath. Say 'Ah' with every out-breath.

◆ *Draw the breath up to the third eye chakra and send it out through your genitals, still breathing through your sex. As usual, the woman leads this changeover.*

◆ *After several minutes, draw up the energy to the crown chakra together.*

◆ *Move into the Shiva–Shakti position now, where the man sits cross-legged on cushions and his partner sits on his lap with her legs wrapped around his waist. Change over to alternate breathing (see page 316). The woman holds her breath while her partner exhales. Then when he next inhales, she exhales, so that he is breathing in her out-breath. She also holds her pelvis still while holding her breath. Once she starts moving her pelvis, they will be tilting back and forward simultaneously.*

◆ *The man inhales your breath through his heart, sending it down through his energy channels and out through his lingam (penis). The woman inhales through her yoni as he exhales through his genitals.*

◆ *Relax into the atmosphere of love and oneness generated by circulating your energy in this way (see pages 357 and 360).*

EXPLORING WOMEN'S PLEASURE ZONES: THE GODDESS SPOT

Even while my mind held back, my body responded joyfully. His touch dispelled my resistance. His caress over-rode my resolve. My thigh longed to grip his waist, my sex hungered to know him.

He entered me deeply, and my love muscle clasped at the soft fullness of him, stroking the head of his penis as he stroked my g-spot. Astride him I was pushing and sliding on him in just the way that most excited me, when without warning I let go into a turbulent melting that left me sheltering in his encircling arms. Was it so easy to reach the orgasm that had always eluded me, because I thought it was somehow outside me? Now I had discovered that an orgasm was about sinking into the way my body met and enclosed his, both active and surrendered at the same time.

Tantrics call the g-spot the goddess spot, acknowledging its role in bringing women to peak states of arousal. This exercise is excellent for women who have difficulty achieving orgasm. Although orgasm is not the aim of Tantric sex, it's important to know that you can achieve it as an expression of your pleasure. This exercise will usually go on to trigger extended sexual orgasm (see page 336).

Give your lover more time for genital pleasure than she's ever had before. This is not foreplay; it is a precursor to learning to give her an orgasm with your hands. You will need to locate your partner's goddess spot once she is fully aroused sexually, as this is when the tissue becomes more sensitive. You do this by exploring the front of her vagina (facing the abdomen) with your finger, until you discover the area that she finds most pleasurable.

The following ritual begins after you've stimulated and relaxed your lover's body with stroking and massage. Once she feels sexually excited she invites you to begin.

Ritual

◆ *The woman lies comfortably with her legs open. Position yourself so that you can talk and maintain eye contact, as well as stimulate her pearl (clitoris) with one hand and yoni with the other.*

◆ *Lightly brush her pubic hair, teasing and gently tweaking the flesh. Caress her thighs and the lips of her vulva as you apply lubricant over the whole area. You can blow over the area, or gently lick. Experiment with different styles of stimulation – and stay with what works well.*

◆ *Use your thumb at the top of her pearl, while your fingers stroke downward. Stroke either side, and along the shaft of the clitoris, or circle around it. Keep your stroke slowly and steady, at the rate of about one stroke each second.*

◆ *When your partner is very excited, slowly slide your middle finger into her vagina. Gently explore the inside of the vagina in every direction, and slowly massage it. The rest of your hand can rest on, or massage, the pubic mound. Vary the depth, speed, and pressure of your finger.*

◆ *With your palm facing up, and the middle finger crooked back toward the palm inside the yoni, move the middle finger in a "come here" gesture. Explore the spongy area*

of tissue just under the pubic bone, behind the clitoris. Move your finger around until you find the pleasurable g-spot.

◆ *Experiment with all sorts of different strokes, changing them gradually rather than rapidly, so that your partner has time to relax into the sensations. When your partner is enjoying what you're doing, continue the same movements for several minutes. If her arousal diminishes, keep your movements gentle until she gets excited again. She can build her own arousal by concentrating on breathing in through her yoni, squeezing her love muscle (see page 234) to draw up the sexual energy into her body. Keep stimulating her pearl in the way that she likes it.*

◆ *A teasing pattern increases arousal. Use several strokes that she finds pleasurable, then repeat them very lightly once or twice before returning to the pleasurable pressure. If she does orgasm, continue to rhythmically stroke the g-spot, but lighten your touch.*

93

EXPLORING MEN'S PLEASURE ZONES: THE PROSTATE

The prostate corresponds to the "g" (goddess) spot in women – they come from the same tissue. Stimulating a man's prostate gives a deeper, more intense and prolonged orgasm. Simultaneously stroking the lingam (penis) and then the area of the prostate produces a high intensity state of arousal. This sacred spot in men is found by pressing deeply into the perineum (midway between the testicles and anus). It can also be reached through the wall of the anus, if your partner enjoys that.

 The aim of this exercise is to explore his pleasure zones, from inside the anus or on the external prostate spot. He can learn to relax his anus while focusing on pleasurable feelings around the prostate area, which helps make orgasm less penis-focused.

Ritual

◆ *Your man leans back on comfortable cushions, with his knees up and legs apart. Sit between his legs so that you have good access to your partner's genitals with both hands, and can maintain eye contact easily.*

◆ *Lubricate his pelvis area and genitals with a good oil or lubricant, while gazing at his face.*

◆ *Arouse him by touching his penis with a variety of different strokes.*

◆ *Play with his scrotum and perineum, the area just behind his testicles, toward his anus. This is called the external prostate or sacred spot.*

◆ *Steady pressure here feels good, or a firm stroking in rhythm with the strokes you're giving his lingam. You can press your thumb into the sacred spot while hooking your finger around his lingam.*

◆ *To build up arousal, you can build up the speed of your rhythmic strokes. He can squeeze his love muscle (see page 60), and use breathing to build up erotic energy. To* slow it down, change and vary the pace and pressure of your strokes.

◆ If you don't want him to ejaculate, gently pull or stretch the testicles. Don't stimulate the head of his penis at this stage - stroke the energy away from the pelvis, especially down his legs and up to his heart area, as you did during the lingam massage.

◆ It is better to explore the anus when your partner is feeling excited, as the sensations are more likely to be pleasurable. However, remember that this exercise is about exploration, rather than giving your partner an intense orgasm. Make sure that you touch him very gently and slowly, as the tissues inside the anus are delicate.

◆ Your fingernails should be short and your hands clean. To insert your finger inside the anus use a rubber protective, called a finger cot, to cover your finger, or a latex glove. Massage the perineum and anus with massage oil, and the rectum with either oil or Vaseline. When he is ready, push the tip of your finger into the inside of the anus, encouraging your partner to take a few deep breaths and focus on relaxation as you do so. Hold your finger just inside the anus until the muscles relax. When he is ready, push your

*finger in a little more, and gently massage the inside of the
anal muscles.*

◆ *While his anus is being explored, your partner relaxes into
the sensations. If he is at all uncomfortable he should ask
you to hold completely still, rather than withdrawing.
When he finds the sensations pleasurable, he can use deep
breathing alternating with panting to heighten his
response. He can also clench the love muscle (see page
232). Gradually reduce the stimulation before he ejaculates, and relax together in a loving embrace.*

94

·◆·

ECSTATIC SEX WITH GODDESS
SPOT STIMULATION

We were dressed in silk kimonos. My lover had lit the candles, put on our favorite sexy tape, and poured me a glass of wine. As I bent forward, he leaned into the nape of my neck. His hot breath excited me. He stroked my body through the kimono.

We exchanged kisses, sucking each other's saliva into our mouths. He bent down before me to lick my yoni. I lay back on some pillows to savor his divine tongue. He stroked my pearl, circling and playing with it, until my juices ran down and he entered me with his finger. He stroked the inside of my vagina, but in spite of my excitement I was not very sensitive to his touch.

When he entered me, his lingam immediately rubbed my g-spot as he came deep inside me. My back supported by pillows, I curled into him. I lay beneath him, rounding my sacrum more and more, curling my thighs and buttocks against his abdomen so that he could reach deep inside.

He was channeling god-like energy though his lingam, driving against my goddess spot. I could feel the deep belly laugh of the goddess's pleasure climbing through my groin and navel. As my orgasm started I relaxed my thighs and felt the waves become more gentle, moving up my body like petals from a lotus flower. As my orgasm went, on these pinky-white petals grew up my body. When they were around my torso, it was as if flames were emerging from the tip of this flower. Although they were red, they felt cool.

 For women, having intercourse with g-spot stimulation increases your pleasure intensely. If you have found that the inside of your vagina is not usually enjoyably sensitive during intercourse, your partner will need to locate your g-spot (see page 324) and then you can both experiment with love-making positions that facilitate the right angle of penetration to suit your anatomy. Learning to stimulate the goddess spot appropriately is necessary to expand sexual pleasure and induce bliss.

Ritual

◆ *Find a way to honor your partner as if he or she were part of the divine couple, Shiva and Shakti (see page 178), for instance by offering flowers, or a candle to symbolize your burning passion.*

◆ *Start with slow breathing, harmonizing with each other. Explore your lover's body with feathers, breath, fingertips, mouth, and tongue.*

◆ *Stimulate each other manually first, moving on to a blended stimulation of both positive and negative sexual poles (see page 300); the tip of the penis and the prostate in men, the clitoris and g-spot in women.*

◆ *During intercourse, the best way for a woman to stimulate her own g-spot with your partner's penis is when you are sitting on top. You can try leaning backward. While on top, pump your love muscle (contract and release the muscles around your vagina and anus several times at the rate of about twice per second). Alternatively, try pumping*

your love muscle and grinding your pelvis against your partner's pubic mound in such a way that it rubs your clitoris or stimulate your clitoris with your hand.

◆ *If you are laying underneath your partner, you need a pillow under your bottom so that your pelvis is rotated up toward his. To increase the depth of his penetration, lay your legs along his torso and chest so that your feet frame his face. Vary the pace and depth of his penetration. Try short deep thrusts – this can be very exiting for you without pushing him over into an orgasm. Or, you can lay in an adaptation of the cat pose, a yoga posture in which you kneel with your buttocks raised in the air, exposing your vulva, your back bowed downward and your head resting on your crossed arms.*

Variation

Imagine milking him with your love muscle squeezing in order to receive his sexual energy. Visualize sending it back to him through your vaginal walls, in order to recirculate it.

The man can pump his own love muscle while his partner orgasms, imagining that you are absorbing her sexual energy through your penis, drawing it into your being.

95

EXTENDED SEXUAL PLEASURE
FOR WOMEN

For the first time, I felt met. It wasn't just the way he
seemed so tuned into my body, nor the gentle sensuality of
his touch. It was the openness of his heart's pure love
pouring out of him. Resting in his arms, I experienced the joy
of feeling deeply loved. My needs were finally met, so I didn't
feel needy; my hunger was satisfied. Stroking my g-spot with
his fingers, I felt the excitement of him softly pushing inside
me, through the tightness of my vagina into the enclosing
embrace deep inside. And how I love it deep, when his
lingam touches a gentle wave of orgasm.

 During their sexual union, the goddess Shakti experiences seven peaks of ecstasy, each peak higher,

stronger, and more powerful than the preceding, until she releases her nectar (female ejaculate). Stimulation of the g-spot during prolonged pleasuring can lead to female ejaculation, the release of liquid described by Tantrics as divine nectar (amrita).

The following exercise explores extended sexual pleasure to prepare you for the sixth stage, a Tantric speciality called "the wave of bliss". The wave of bliss involves expanding extended sexual pleasure into an altered state of consciousness, using the breathing and visualization techniques we've been exploring throughout the book. This can transform sex totally, taking it to another realm.

Prepare a sacred space in the room you will use to make love (see page 38). Find a way to honor your beloved as a goddess, by offering her a flower in water, or a floating candle. You may give her a present, or read her a poem.

Bow to her, visualizing her as a gorgeous goddess whom you are honored to make love to.

The Ritual

◆ *Start with a sensory awakening ritual (such as pages 136–47) or massage.*

◆ *Stroke each other's body with love and care. Slow, delicate touch heightens arousal. Pay attention to her whole body, don't rush for her sexual organs.*

◆ *When she is aroused, rub almond oil all over her sex, including the outer and inner lips, clitoris, entrance to the vagina, and external anus. Gently play with her pubic hair, and explore her genitalia with different pressures and strokes. Tease the pearl (clitoris) by brushing it and circling around it using one, two or more fingers. Tantrics respect the clitoris as the gateway to sexual pleasure, and learn to arouse it during rituals honoring the yoni.*

◆ *Experiment with light, delicate strokes, about once a second, maintaining the rhythm your partner enjoys. Slowly vary your strokes. Encourage her to roll her pelvis around, moving or arching her back and squeezing her love muscle (see page 320) as you pleasure her.*

◆ *When she asks you to enter her, slip one or two fingers inside to stroke her g-spot, which is in the front and upward in the vagina – one and a half or two inches inside. Once you've found the area that feels intensely pleasurable, rub it once each second.*

◆ *She may like to stimulate her own clitoris as you are stroking her g-spot.*

◆ *When your partner starts to orgasm, switch attention to stimulating her vagina, rhythmically rubbing her g-spot area with one or two fingers. If your fingers are hooked upward, rubbing the top wall of her vagina where it feels extremely pleasurable, this increases her enjoyment and the depth of orgasm. As she begins the contractions of her orgasm, rhythmically stroke the inside of her vagina - the g-spot may appreciate a lot of pressure at this time. Maintain the same rhythm that worked with the clitoris — again, about one stroke per second. As you continue stimulating, she may go into deeper pelvic contractions. As they lessen, lighten your stimulation of the g-spot and try to stimulate her clitoris again until you feel her orgasm building again. Stimulate her g-spot through the contractions.*

◆ *When her pelvis contracts in orgasm, lighten your touch, then switch back to stimulating her pearl. You can sustain her high level of arousal and, eventually, produce multiple orgasms by alternating between the vagina and clitoris for at least another quarter of an hour, or more.*

96

EXTENDED SEXUAL PLEASURE
FOR MEN

Extending sexual pleasure means really experiencing the full potential of your sex – it is much more than being able to come as quickly as possible. During extended sexual pleasuring, men learn to peak and plateau again without going into orgasm. By focusing on the moment between orgasm and ejaculation, you can extend and deepen your experience of ejaculation. When you separate your orgasm from ejaculation you become multi-orgasmic, experiencing the internal muscle contractions that sex researchers term the "valley" orgasm, a deeper and more satisfying type of climax.

In this ritual, you learn to expand the length of your orgasmic contractions from seconds to minutes or even longer, maintaining a high level of arousal without physically ejaculating. In this way, you can enjoy making love more often and for longer.

Ritual

Before starting this exercise, jointly commit to delaying orgasm for as long as possible, in order to lengthen it when it does occur. Agree on the tactics that you will use if you tell your partner that you need to stop yourself ejaculating.

Variation

Stimulate yourself to the very edge of orgasm, when contractions start at the base of your penis, around your prostate and anus. By paying attention to these contractions you can build them in intensity so that you can orgasm repeatedly without ejaculating. Once you can self-pleasure for half an hour without ejaculating, you'll be able to go on as long as you want with your partner.

◆ *Your man leans back on comfortable cushions, with his legs apart. Position yourself lying between his legs with your head on one thigh so you can stimulate his penis with one hand and rub the area of the external prostate with the other.*

◆ *Start by lubricating his pelvis area and genitals with massage oil or lubricant and play with his penis to arouse him (see lingam massage, page 252).*

- *After at least a quarter of an hour, start playing with his scrotum and perineum (the area over his prostate, or sacred spot). Stroke firmly in rhythm with the way you're touching his penis, or try steady pressure with your thumb. If he enjoys anal stimulation, gently rub the internal prostate spot – usually the length of between one to two knuckles inside the anus, on the upper wall of the rectum. Your partner will be able to tell you where it feels especially pleasurable, and what sort of pressure he enjoys.*

- *When he gets very excited, switch back to his lingam. Swap between his penis and prostate to give him waves of pleasure. To build arousal, increase the speed of your rhythmic strokes. He can squeeze his love muscle (see page 56), and alternate rapid and deep breathing.*

- *Gently pull or stretch the testicles if he looks like he's becoming very aroused. To cool him down stop stimulating his penis, while he uses breathing to disperse energy towards his heart, slowing the contractions right down.*

- *To avoid imminent orgasm, intensify the muscular tension in your love muscles as though straining to start a bowel movement. Then completely relax those same muscles to disperse contractions.*

◆ *Together, build up to high levels of arousal, then come down again several more times. After a while, you'll be able to maintain high levels of arousal without needing to ejaculate, and experience a series of orgasms similar to those experienced by multi-orgasmic women. Without panting and jerking in preparation for climax, you can melt into a state of intense pleasure, choosing whether or not to orgasm. Your lingam becomes extremely sensitive: a single drop of lubricant, a light blowing breath, or the slightest touch of a tongue gives intense pleasure.*

◆ *During this experience Shiva, focus on drawing up the blissful sensations from your genitals through your chakras (energy centers) into your heart, and eventually your crown chakra.*

97

RELAXING INTO ORGASM

I relaxed into my feeling of sensual excitement, using the pelvic floor muscle (love muscle or fire muscle) to spread my arousal through my whole body. I felt I had melted into her. She is my soul mate. When our souls are joined, I feel at one with the universe.

 Staying relaxed while sexually aroused allows you to receive erotic energy from your partner. The eroticism generated can suffuse your whole body. This expands your excitement into whole-body pleasure, a pre-requisite for whole-body orgasm.

In order to build up toward an orgasm, most people tense the muscles, especially around the thighs and pelvis. In energetic terms, tension involves contracting inward, reducing the ability of energy to flow through your body. Relaxation involves expansion – when you are deeply relaxed, your erotic energy spreads from your genitals into the whole body. Tantrics encourage expansion by visualizing the sexual energy permeating other energy centers, or chakras (see page 52) in your body, especially the heart and the crown.

This ritual allows you to expand your sexual energy by sinking into a state of deep relaxation, breathing deeply yet slowly. As you soften your body, you soften and open your heart to your beloved. Concentrate on the movement of energy generated by your heart connection, as well as your erotic excitement, as you make love.

Before starting to make love, prepare your bodies with erotic touch (see page 48), awakening the senses (see pages 136–49), or an energy massage (see page 120).

Ritual

This exercise starts when you are nearing orgasm during love-making. At the moment just before orgasm, when you feel your muscles are about to contract, you learn to extend this moment by relaxing into your orgasm. If you can't reach orgasm without tensing your buttocks and thighs, try to let one or two contractions occur in your usual way, and then stop making an effort to reach orgasm. Relax and fall into the pleasurable sensations.

◆ *After a couple of waves of orgasmic contractions, help yourself to relax by breathing slowly and deeply. Relax your abdominal muscles as you breathe. Enjoy the sensations without trying to prolong them.*

◆ *Imagine yourself hovering on the edge of your pleasure, rather than plunging over the edge. Feel yourself on the edge for sometime.*

◆ *Take turns during love-making. One of you pleasure the other right to the brink of orgasm, then swap roles just before orgasm. Let yourself come back from the edge and then build sexual excitement repeatedly up to the brink again. Do this several times.*

◆ *Once you and your partner become attuned to one another, you will no longer think about who is pleasuring who, and who is on the edge. You will both relax into a floating state of intense pleasure in your sensations, which prolongs your enjoyment. Float into a gentle bliss together, wrapped in your mutual love.*

Variation

Practice this when self-pleasuring alone (see page 270).

98

NON-DOING IN LOVE-MAKING

We spent hours making love, and then stopping to explore each other's bodies further, exploring different feelings and physical sensations. I surrendered to the process instead of trying to stay in control. We'd stop and lay together, with him still inside me, looking at each other, cuddling and talking. I felt a deep sense of peace, and of love. It was very joyful, and blissful, whether we were having intercourse or laying exhausted together. Neither of us wanted to break it. I was having little orgasms throughout our love-making, and eventually after hours, he'd have an orgasm, and we would get some rest, feeling fully satisfied in a way I'd never felt before. My orgasm seemed pulled out of me slowly, rather than rushing out. I understand more about the softness of opening out to him, and of slowness and sensitivity.

Tantric sex involves coming together, rather than coming. Non-doing depends on letting go of your expectations – not being goal-oriented, or striving to increase your excitement levels, or rushing toward orgasm. You need to empty yourself of expectations in order to allow yourselves to explore whatever arises between you. Don't worry about losing excitement; just trust that another great experience will be pleasurable.

Non-doing in Tantric love-making involves intercourse, but without striving for an orgasm through active movement or friction. Giving up your attachment to orgasm paradoxically allows you to be fully in the present moment and experience more pleasure. In this ritual, you explore the subtle sensations produced by small movements of your pelvis, your love muscles, and altering your breathing. Immerse yourself in your whole body sensations, and use this sexual energy to nourish your heart and soul connection with your lover.

It is important to focus on the emotional and sexual connection with your partner. Visualize your heart opening with love throughout love-making.

Ritual

◆ *Use blended stimulation of the pearl (clitoris) or lingam (penis), plus nipples, earlobes, toes, feet, back of the knees, and inside of the elbows. While doing this, spread the energy from the genitals toward the area of the heart with light massage strokes.*

◆ *Frequently pause while stimulating your partner to allow them to bask in the sensations. Hold one hand over their genitals and the other over their heart while doing this. Gaze at them lovingly, enjoying their pleasure.*

◆ *Penetration is usually soft penetration. To encourage your penis to fill with blood, when it falls out your partner can create a ring with her finger at the base of your penis, while stimulating the tip with her mouth or other hand.*

◆ *The woman can massage her vulva with her partner's soft lingam, and then guide the soft lingam into the entrance of her vagina. This feels particularly nice while sitting in the Shiva–Shakti posture (see page 180).*

◆ *Alternatively, the man can rub his penis around his lover's pearl. When it becomes more erect, rub it into the entrance of the vagina, swirling around the entrance and back up to circle the pearl. For soft penetration try the*

350

scissors position, where you face each other, with the woman placing one hip over her partner's waist and the other between his thighs, so that he can enter her vagina easily.

◆ Start to make love any way you like. As you feel your excitement climbing, stop moving and lay still with the lingam inside the yoni (vagina), just experiencing the sensations without having to create more. Use the minimal movement you need just to maintain an erection. Don't worry about losing your erection, as you can easily re-stimulate it.

◆ You can alternate this total relaxation with squeezing your love muscle (see page 234) together, or use gentle stroking for pleasurable sensation anywhere on the body.

◆ If an urge to orgasm or ejaculate arises, let go of it. Allow your sexual centers to penetrate each other and create a bridge for the exchange of energies. Surrender yourselves to however the process unfolds itself.

◆ Stay relaxed and maintain eye contact throughout love-making. Maintain your awareness of your heart center (chakra), using any of the breathing exercises you feel comfortable with (see pages, 308 and 312).

99

CIRCULAR BREATHING DURING
LOVE-MAKING

I tasted his tongue on my upper lip. He inhaled my breath,
renewing it and then returning it to me. We continued like
this for half an hour, offering each other our recycled breath
as if it were the elixir of life. Through this breathing, inhaling
each other, we seemed to be incorporating each other into
our cells. The heady alkalosis sent my head spinning into a
swoon. We drove through the night with fireworks exploding
around us. It was a bigger high than anything I'd ever
experienced; I felt euphoric for weeks.

In this ritual, you create bliss by joining your physical
and energy-bodies in a complete melting embrace.
With your genitals and mouths joined together energy is

sealed within you as one body, creating a profoundly nourishing intimacy. As you make love, focus on the transfer of vital energy that occurs as you exchange breaths.

Ritual

◆ *Sitting in Shiva–Shakti posture, where the man sits cross-legged on cushions and his partner sits on his lap with her legs around his waist, use chakra breathing to create a fire in your joint pelvis. The man can start with the active breath, which involves breathing out through his genitals and in through his heart. The woman starts with the receptive breath, breathing in through her genitals, and out through her heart (see page 316).*

◆ *At any point the woman can invite the man to enter her. Make love in a gentle, loving way. Focus on the energy qualities of your partner's genitals (see page 274) as you send and receive breath through them. Settle into an alternate pattern of breathing, in which the woman holds her breath while her partner exhales. Then when he next inhales, she exhales, so that he is breathing in her out-breath. She also holds her pelvis still while holding her breath. As she starts moving her pelvis forward, he tilts his back with his in-breath. You both rock your pelvises back and forward together.*

◆ *The man inhales your breath through his heart and sends it down through his energy channels and out through his lingam. The woman inhales through her yoni as he exhales through his genitals. Relax into love.*

◆ *Bring the breath up to the area of your throat and mouth. Cover your partner's lips with your own, completely sealing the breath. The man inhales through his mouth as the woman exhales through hers. Then the man exhales as the woman inhales through her mouth. Do this for up to ten to fifteen minutes. Occasionally inhale through your nostrils to bring in some fresh air.*

◆ *With your mouths together, continue this circular breathing. As your partner exhales, breathe in their warm breath, and imagine it traveling all the way down to your genitals. As you breathe out, send the sexual energy out through your tilted pelvis onto your partner's genitals. From there your partner will draw the energy up to their mouth. With your mouths together you become one energy-body, circulating energy internally. Touch the tip of your partner's tongue with your own.*

◆ *You can then imagine that you're circulating the energy through your genitals and your third eye center, or chakra (see page 311), rather than your mouth. When you're both feeling very aroused and on the verge of orgasm, close your eyes. To seal the energy in your body rather than release it in orgasm, roll your eyes upward focusing inwards on your third eye, and squeeze your love muscle (see page 230), holding them as you both hold your breath. One of you will be holding your breath in, the other will be holding without any air in their lungs. When it's no longer comfortable, take a breath, and your partner will exhale, and hold. Relax the rest of your body, and just allow the energy to stream upward through your body.*

◆ *Remain quite still for several minutes. Allow yourself to breathe naturally, taking as many breaths through your nostrils as you need.*

◆ *Then move your bodies and pelvises to build up erotic excitement again, focusing on one partner inhaling as the other exhales, mouths sealing this exchange of energy with sealed lips. Now you can circulate the energy right up to your crown chakra, enclosing your whole energy system within one circulating ball of bliss.*

100

THE WAVE OF BLISS

The lotus flower, the sex organ of the partner, is an ocean filled with bliss. This lotus flower is also a transparent place, where the thought of enlightenment can rise up. When it is united with the scepter, the male organ, their mixture is compared to the elixir made from myrrh and nutmeg. From their union a pure knowledge arises, which explains the nature of all existence.

KALACHAKRA TANTRA

 The wave of bliss is referred to by a founding father of Tantrism, Saraha. The essence of Tantra involves relishing sexual experience for the experience of bliss it offers. Sexual pleasure is a gateway to divine bliss. Sexual union is used as a direct pathway to a spiritual awakening, because during sex we are more open to direct experience of the bliss that is all around us. During sacred sex you enter the flow of energy. This exercise will bring you into the realm of sacred sex.

Ritual

◆ *When you are both highly aroused by your sexual play, sit in Shiva–Shakti position, the posture of sacred union. Make yourselves comfortable with plenty of cushions to support you both. The man sits in an open lotus position legs loosely crossed with your partner on your lap, her legs wrapped around your waist. If this is uncomfortable, she can support her own weight by squatting over your penis.*

◆ *Gaze lovingly at each other. Open your hearts and let your love flow.*

◆ *When your mouths are touching, and your lingam (penis) is inside her yoni (vagina), a circuit of energy is created. Your joined bodies form a yantra (see page 226), a posture which potentizes the energy created by your merged energy bodies. Intensify the energy by sealing your mouths or squeezing the love muscles, then circulate it between you.*

- *Start to breathe together. Maintain a gentle, even rhythm. Follow your partner's pattern of breathing. Imagine you are breathing in through your heart, absorbing each other's love, and out through your genitals (see page 308).*
- *Allow your pelvis to rock gently back and forth as you breathe. Tilt your pelvis slightly forward as you breathe inward, and backward as you breathe out, letting the energy stream from your genitals into those of your partner.*
- *Practice squeezing your love muscle (see page 56) with each inhalation, and relaxing it with every exhalation. With the love muscle squeeze, hold the energy in your base chakra, releasing it when you relax the muscle.*
- *Pull the energy up with the love muscle, squeezing it to create an energy flow up the inner flute (see page 234). Squeeze it as you breathe in, relax it as you breathe out and allow the breath to return out through the base of your spine.*
- *Visualize your sexual desire as a flame climbing from the base chakra into your pelvis, encompassing both of you. The fire meditation fuels your erotic charge as you draw the energy up through each successive chakra. You should be able to feel energy streaming up your body, from your*

pelvis, as the sexual charge you are creating becomes more
intense.

◆ *As you reach the top chakra, on the crown of the head,*
begin to breathe alternately. When you change to alter-
nate breathing you will notice that both your pelvises are
now tilting forward at the same time, and backward at
the same time — when you breathe out. Still sitting in
Shiva–Shakti, the woman starts with the inner breath,
breathing in through her genitals, and out through her
heart, while you follow the male breath, which is breath-
ing out through your genitals and in through your heart.
You can feel the breath of your partner coming out of their
mouth. Breathe it in, inhaling their loving energy.

Variation

At this stage you can join your mouths together and exchange
breath (see previous exercise, page 352). Visualize the divine
lovers, shiva and shakti, above you (see page 178) and let their
emanations rain down on you.

•◆•

101

MAITHUNA: TANTRIC RITUAL SEX

I always thought that opening the inner flute would be cathartic, and like an experience of fireworks, but instead it was incredibly gentle and soft, and went on forever. It's not like a powerful surge of energy, but a streaming of very fine energy without any bars at all. I felt my lover's energy course through my body and come out of my head and then back into his body. Every cell in my body was vibrating at a high frequency. I felt totally peaceful and harmonious... there was no sense of time. It was like the highest form of meditation I've ever experienced.

 Maithuna refers to ritual sex. Give your love-making its full importance by making it into a ritual that you can extend, explore, and develop. By using ritual, you are working with the potent energy created through your loving relationship. In deliberately making sex sacred, sexuality becomes a doorway to discovering your soul. When you consciously breathe sexual energy into your higher energy centers, your sexuality and spirituality become mutually completing aspects of your being.

Celebrate the purpose of your relationship, which is to open yourself to ecstasy. To connect your sexual energy with your heart and soul, become aware of how energy moves through your body in states of high arousal. Enter into these subtle erotic sensations during love-making. You can facilitate the flow of energy using breathing and visualization to enhance your orgasm. Ecstasy is not just about peak experiences. It also means moving away from stasis and into flow.

Experience a whole-body orgasm, expanding orgasm from a pleasurable physical climax to a state of rapture and heart connection with your lover. During love-making, focus on the quality of the connection between you rather than whether you're "performing" well. Make love with your heart and soul.

Ritual

◆ *Create a sensual ambience with pleasing music. Choose tranquil sounds that slowly build to an insistent beat – a rhythm that you can make love to.*

◆ *Start by connecting with your partner. Sit opposite each other and gaze at them with an open heart (see page 198).*

◆ *Bring your breathing in tune with each other. Focus on opening your root or base chakra, at the base of the spine (see page 42), arousing your sexual center. Then bring this sexual energy up to the heart, offering it to your partner.*

◆ *Move into the Shakti–Shiva position where you are sitting with your legs wrapped around each other. As you breathe slowly and deeply, in a synchronous rhythm, focus on directing the energy to your third eye (brow) chakra together as your breath enlivens it, then your crown chakra.*

◆ *Build sexual arousal with pelvic rocking and squeezing the love muscle (see page 322). Once you are both highly aroused, the woman places her partner's penis between the lips of her vulva. While it's massaging your clitoris, concentrate on the energy emanating from his penis, then open your legs to receive his lingam, when you feel ready.*

- *During intercourse remain focused on the breathing. Prolong your pleasure by taking time. Take breaks in your love-making. Your love-making gets more intense each time you start up again.*
- *Visualize your breath swinging down all the energy centers in your body, and up through those of your partner – in a U shape linked by your pelvises (see page 316). Share your breath by inhaling your partner's exhaled air, sending you into an even more heady state (see page 354). While you are circulating your breath, focus on the energy streaming up your body from your genitals, and relax into a whole-body orgasm.*

GLOSSARY

Amrita Sacred nectar that results from love-making.

Anjala mudra A hand gesture used to honor and welcome a deity.

Aum This sacred sound (om) is considered to be the sound the universe makes in its natural state of constant vibration. It is used as a mantra to attune oneself with the energy vibrations of the cosmos.

Bindu The moment of transition between conscious and unconscious states; the central energy-spot of a yantra.

Chakra Literally, "wheel". It represents a concentration of energy in our subtle energy-body. The principal chakras are located in seven centers on the physical body.

Hatha yoga A traditional yoga system that uses physical postures and breathing techniques to move energy around the body and balance opposite energies; Ha means "sun", and tha, "moon".

Ida An energy channel on the left side of the body that spirals around the sushumna, or central energy channel.

Kundalini This energy lies sleeping in the chakra at the base of the spine. It is depicted as a snake, with her body coiled three-and-a-half times around a lingam. It is a symbol of the interconnectedness of the Shakti and Shiva principles.

Lingam Literally meaning "mark", the erect phallus symbolizes Shiva consciousness, transcendence.

Mandala means "circle". It describes an outdoor earthen platform used for rituals, as well as a ritual space, a circle of friends, and an assembly. As an enclosed sacred space, mandala also refers to the yoni in Tantric usage.

Mantra A sacred word or phrase used in meditation to focus awareness.

Mudra is a ritual gesture in devotional worship, a hand gesture using the hands that invokes the presence of a deity. In Tantric Buddhism it refers to the female partner in couple rituals.

Mula bhanda Meaning "root lock", this is an important seal used to hold sexual energies in the body so they can be circulated internally. The pubococcygeal (love) muscle is squeezed in order to prevent ejaculation and to raise sexual energy.

Nadi sodhana Meaning "clearing the channels", this is a detoxifying yoga exercise.

Namaste is a Hindu form of greeting where the hands are held together as if praying. In Tantra, it is used to mean "I honor you as an aspect of the divine."

Nidra yoga A yoga technique that uses auto-suggestion to access the higher consciousness.

Pingala An energy channel on the right side of the body that spirals around the sushumna, or central channel.

Prana Vital energy; the breath of life.

Puja A ritual of worship or devotion.

Shakti A Hindu goddess. Used as a generic term for goddess meaning divine female, or goddess energy in Tantrism.

Shakti-Kundalini The serpent power located at the base of the spine, which is considered our own personal storehouse of Shakti energy.

Shiva A Hindu god, Shakti's consort. The divine male energy in Tantrism.

Shri yantra This yantra is dedicated to a form of the goddess, Tripura Sundari. The design is made of five downward-pointing triangles, which represent Shakti energy, and four upward-pointing triangles, which symbolize Shiva energy.

Soma The water of life, which arises when sperm is transformed during love-making.

Sukhasana Easy pose. This is an easy posture for meditation where the legs are crossed with each foot under the opposite knee.

Sushumna The body's central energy channel.

Yantra A yantra is a visual representation of inner and outer energy processes in geometric form. These patterns are used as tools in meditation to help the mediator align themselves with appropriate energy flows, and they represent the energies associated with the deity.

Yoni In Hinduism and Tantra the female genitals stand for Shakti energy, or immanence. Yoni is a Sanskrit word for the vagina that connotes sacred space, or sanctum.

ACKNOWLEDGEMENTS

Many fabulous teachers and researchers of Tantra have inspired me. My heartfelt thanks in particular to SkyDancing UK teacher John Hawken, who initiated me into the mystery of Tantra. John's teacher, Margo Anand, has written two excellent workbooks, *The Art of Sexual Ecstasy* and *The Art of Sexual Magic* (both Thorsons). *Sexual Secrets* by Nik Douglas and Penny Slinger (Destiny Books) provides a fascinating encyclopaedic compendium of Tantric perspectives and teachings. *Zen Flesh, Zen Bones* (Penguin) contains an early translation by Paul Reps of profoundly simple meditation insights offered in the *Vijnana Bhairava*. And finally the beautiful images collected by Phillip Rawson in *Tantra: The Indian Cult of Ecstasy* (Thames and Hudson) were a further inspiration for our illustrations.

INDEX